REFERENCE

Form 178 rev. 01-07

Solar Power

Clay Farris Naff, *Book Editor*

Christine Nasso, *Publisher*
Elizabeth Des Chenes, *Managing Editor*

GREENHAVEN PRESS
An imprint of Thomson Gale, a part of The Thomson Corporation

Detroit • New York • San Francisco • New Haven, Conn. • Waterville, Maine • London

Picture Credits:
Cover: Getty Images; AFP/Getty Images, 90-91; Ariadne Van Zandbergen/Lonely Planet Images, 67; © Bettmann/CORBIS, 19; © Bohemian Nomad Picturemakers/CORBIS, 51; © David Butow/SABA/CORBIS, 107; David Else/Lonely Planet Images, 105; © Eye Ubiquitous/CORBIS, 84; Galleria degli Uffizi, Florence, Italy/Bridgeman Art Library, 17; © George Steinmetz/CORBIS, 36; Getty Images, 74, 81, 93, 95; Hermitage, St. Petersburg, Russia/Bridgeman Art Library, 22; Hulton Archive/Getty Images, 15; Hulton-Deutsch Collection/CORBIS, 20; © Jim Sugar/CORBIS, 12-13; © Klaus Hackenberg/zefa/CORBIS, 45; © Lester Lefkowitz/CORBIS, 9; Michael Springer/Bloomberg News/Landov, 87; NASA, 35, 97; Picture History, 27; Private Collection/Bridgeman Art Library, 24; © Reuters/CORBIS, 10; Reuters/Landov, 89; © Richard Hamilton Smith/CORBIS, 77; © Richard T. Nowitz/CORBIS, 64; © Robert Vos/epa/CORBIS, 43; © Roger Ressmeyer/CORBIS, 56; Steve Zmina, 32, 39, 40, 48, 54, 57, 60, 78, 101, 108; © Strauss/Curtis/CORBIS, 68; © The Cover Story/CORBIS, 72

ISBN-13: 978-0-7377-3565-9
ISBN-10: 0-7377-3565-1

Library of Congress Control Number: 2006933700

Printed in the United States of America

SOC
Contents

Foreword   6

Introduction   8

Chapter 1: The Development of Solar Power

1. **A Brief History of Solar Energy**   16
   Lucy Cogan

   Ancient people throughout the world made use of the
   sun's rays to heat homes.

2. **How Solar Technology Developed in the**   21
   Nineteenth Century
   Charles Smith

   The director of a sustainable development program
   explains that during the second half of the nineteenth
   century, scientists and engineers refined methods to
   capture and use solar energy.

3. **Discovering How to Turn the Sun's Rays into**   30
   Electricity
   John Perlin

   The development of photovoltaic cells enabled scientists to
   turn solar energy into electricity.

4. **How Today's Solar Technology Works**   38
   Union of Concerned Scientists

   An organization representing scientists concerned about
   the environment explains how the sun's rays can be put
   to work to heat homes and businesses and to generate
   electricity.

Chapter 2: Is Solar Power Viable?

1. **Solar Power Can Make America Energy Independent**   46
   Liz Borkowski

   Solar power can wean America from dependence on fossil fuels and thereby slow global warming.

2. **Solar Power Cannot Make America Energy Independent**   52
   Mike Oliver and John Hospers

   An engineer and a political philosopher argue that solar power is too inefficient to meet America's energy needs.

3. **Solar Power Can Benefit Rich Nations**   59
   Robert F. Service

   If developed nations invest in solar technology, they can meet future energy needs and protect the environment.

4. **Solar Power Is Best Suited for Poor Nations**   66
   Nicholas Thompson and Ricardo Bayon

   Solar power is most viable in rural areas of poor nations, which lack access to a national electrical grid.

Chapter 3: The Future of Solar Energy

1. **American Homes Will Use More Solar Energy**   75
   Joe Provey

   Falling prices for solar cells and rising prices for electricity provided by burning coal or gas will fuel a boom in home solar power systems.

2. **Improved Solar Water Heaters Could Lead to Solar Air Conditioning**   83
   John Colmey

   A Malaysian inventor's new design for solar water heating makes hot water available to people in developing countries. It also could make possible solar-powered air conditioning.

3. Solar and Hydrogen Energy Will Power Future Homes   88
   David G. Schieren

   Someday, homes will be powered by hydrogen made from solar energy.

4. Satellites Will Supply the Earth with Solar Energy   94
   Ralph H. Nansen

   An aeronautical engineer describes his vision for a gigantic solar-power satellite that would turn the sun's energy into electricity, which would be beamed down to Earth for use in homes, businesses, and factories.

5. Solar Energy Will Make Drinking Water Safe in Remote Areas   103
   Trudy C. Rolla

   An environmental health specialist examines how solar energy is being used to kill pathogens in water. Solar boxes and stills can greatly improve the health of the world's poorest people.

Facts About Solar Power   111

Glossary   113

Chronology   116

For Further Reading   120

Index   124

About the Editor   128

Foreword

The wind farm at Altamont Pass in Northern California epitomizes many people's idea of wind power: Hundreds of towering white turbines generate electricity to power homes, factories, and businesses. The spinning turbine blades call up visions of a brighter future in which clean, renewable energy sources replace dwindling and polluting fossil fuels. The blades also kill over a thousand birds of prey each year. Every energy source, it seems, has its price.

The bird deaths at Altamont Pass make clear an unfortunate fact about all energy sources, including renewables: They have downsides. People want clean, abundant energy to power their modern lifestyles, but few want to pay the costs associated with energy production and use. Oil, coal, and natural gas contain high amounts of energy, but using them produces pollution. Commercial solar energy facilities require hundreds of acres of land and thus must be located in rural areas. Expensive and ugly transmission lines must then be run from the solar plants to the cities that need power. Producing hydrogen for fuel involves the use of dirty fossil fuels, tapping geothermal energy depletes ground water, and growing biomass for fuel ties up land that could be used to grow food. Hydroelectric power has become increasingly unpopular because dams flood vital habitats and kill wildlife and plants. Perhaps most controversial, nuclear power plants produce highly dangerous radioactive waste. People's reluctance to pay these environmental costs can be seen in the results of a 2006 Center for Economic and Civic Opinion poll. When asked how much they would support a power plant in their neighborhood, 66 percent of respondents said they would oppose it.

Many scientists warn that fossil fuel use creates emissions that threaten human health and cause global warming. Moreover, numerous scientists claim that fossil fuels are running out. As a result of these concerns, many nations have begun to revisit the energy sources that first powered human enterprises. In his 2006 State of the Union speech, U.S. president George W. Bush announced that since 2001 the United States has spent "$10 billion to develop cleaner, cheaper, and more reliable alternative energy sources," such as biomass and wind power. Despite Bush's positive rhetoric, many critics contend that the renewable energy sources he refers to are still as inefficient as they ever were and cannot possibly power modern economies. As Jerry Taylor and Peter Van Doren of the Cato Institute note, "The market share for non-hydro renewable energy . . . has languished between 1 and 3 percent for decades." Controversies such as this have been a constant throughout the history of humanity's search for the perfect energy source.

Greenhaven Press's Fueling the Future series explores this history. Each volume in the series traces the development of one energy source, and investigates the controversies surrounding its environmental impact and its potential to power humanity's future. The anthologies provide a variety of selections written by scientists, environmental activists, industry leaders, and government experts. Volumes also contain useful research tools, including an introductory essay providing important context, and an annotated table of contents that enables students to locate selections of interest easily. In addition, each volume includes an index, chronology, bibliography, glossary, and a Facts About section, which lists useful information about each energy source. Other features include numerous charts, graphs, and cartoons, which offer additional avenues for learning important information about the topic.

Fueling the Future volumes provide students with important resources for learning about the energy sources upon which human societies depend. Although it is easy to take energy for granted in developed nations, this series emphasizes how energy sources are also problematic. The U.S. Energy Information Administration calls energy "essential to life." Whether scientists will be able to develop the energy sources necessary to sustain modern life is the vital question explored in Greenhaven Press's Fueling the Future series.

Introduction

Like any source of energy, solar power has advantages and disadvantages. On the one hand, it is ubiquitous, clean, and inexhaustible. Ancient people made use of this plentiful energy supply to warm their homes, extract salt from water, and preserve food. Today, solar energy is used to generate electricity without harmful emissions. On the other hand, solar power's considerable disadvantages have prevented it from being a serious rival to coal, natural gas, and nuclear power. One drawback to solar power is that its energy is diffuse, making it difficult to collect enough sunlight to be useful. Solar energy is also inconstant—during cloudy days and nighttime, no solar energy can be collected. Added to these disadvantages are the limitations inherent in the technology used to capture solar energy. The typical solar cell converts no more than 15 percent of the sunlight it receives into electricity. All of these drawbacks have a natural consequence: Electricity generated by solar energy costs more than electricity produced by conventional energy sources. Typically, utilities relying on coal, nuclear power, and natural gas for generation produce electricity for between six and eight cents a kilowatt hour. Solar generation costs as much as thirty-five cents per kilowatt hour.

Given these drawbacks, it may seem surprising that in the first few years of the twenty-first century there has been a global move toward solar generation. Whether this is a fad or a permanent trend has yet to be determined, but what is clear are the reasons why solar has become the center of so much attention.

A Solar Boom

During the last few decades, as energy needs have increased, the world has become painfully aware that fossil fuels are an exhaustible resource. At the same time, many scientists have begun warning that the greenhouse gases released by fossil fuel use are beginning to alter the climate. Evidence of global warming has become harder to ignore as Arctic glaciers retreat and record high temperatures prevail.

Together, these factors have inspired a search for alternative energy sources. This interest in alternatives has come at a time when solar energy technologies have become more efficient and affordable. Many experts believe that solar power may be a significant energy contributor in the future. In February 2006 *Business Week* reporter John Carey noted, "The solar power industry has been on a tear, growing at more than 30% per year for the last six years. It's poised to reach a surprising milestone within two years, when it will gobble up more silicon for its

Solar power is an abundant source of energy on bright, sunny days.

electricity-generating panels than semiconductor makers use in all their [computer] chips and devices."[1] With energy prices rising, the trend toward solar may accelerate. According to the U.S. Department of Energy, sales of photovoltaic cells leaped by 66 percent during 2004.

The rush to embrace solar energy is a global phenomenon, with both poor and affluent nations participating. *Electronics Weekly* reporter David Manners observes, "Many governments, including those of Germany, Japan, Italy, Spain and California have provided incentives to kick-start demand for solar power and some Asian governments are considering similar measures."[2] In developing nations implementation has been sporadic,

Solar power can provide energy to villages such as this one in Tanzania, Africa, that do not have access to electric grids.

but there is widespread enthusiasm for the technology. To understand why, consider this: More than 80 percent of the people in African nations live in villages without access to electric grids. However, electricity can be generated for home use by installing solar panels on villagers' roofs. Many commentators believe that the increased use of solar energy in developing countries will improve the quality of life for the world's poorest people. African journalist Kwabena Osei writes, "I will be calling on African leaders and captains of industry . . . to utilize this vast amount of free energy for the benefit of our people and environment. If we do so, it will undoubtedly lead to the 'second liberation' of our continent."[3]

A Passing Fancy?

Despite the excitement over solar power, many critics believe that solar's popularity is little more than a fad. As they point out, the drawbacks of solar energy persist. Because of solar energy's inefficiency, off-the-grid solar-powered homes remain rare, although a growing number of homeowners are supplementing their heating and electrical power with solar panels installed on their roofs. Grand schemes for using solar energy in new ways, such as for transportation, have largely failed. Even many of those working to develop such technology are pessimistic. Dave Barber, project manager for the University of Missouri's solar-car team, laments, "The majority of the public thinks [making a solar car is] a possibility because they see us doing it. I hate to burst their bubble, but it's probably not going to happen."[4]

While the failure of innovative solar technologies is disheartening for fans of solar energy, the far more serious problem is that solar electricity generation is still expensive. For solar energy to play a significant role in the energy mix, it must generate large quantities of inexpensive electricity for the utility grid. Critics point out that the cost of solar generation still exceeds that of conventional coal or nuclear-powered generators by at least fivefold. What is more, the dilute nature of sunlight means that to achieve significant levels of power, solar collectors have to cover huge areas of land. Many people concerned with the environment dislike the idea of so much land covered by unsightly solar panels. In his book *The Solar Fraud: Why Solar Energy Won't Run the World,* author Howard C. Hayden concludes that scientists and engineers "recognize that solar energy—using all conceivable technologies—will not be adequate to run an industrialized world."[5]

Innovation May Be Key

There is no denying that solar energy has limitations. However, solar-power advocates believe that deepening energy insecurity and technological solutions will make the use of solar energy more viable in the future. Perhaps the most important thing solar power has going for it is the belief that electricity produced by conventional means will continue to get more expensive. A growing number of people are buying home solar kits with the expectation that their investment will pay off within a reasonable period of time as prices rise for electricity produced using finite fossil fuels. At a cost of between five thousand and ten thousand dollars for a home-installed unit, solar is affordable to many homeowners. Homeowners also can get significant rebates on their purchase of solar panels, and they can even earn money feeding any surplus electricity their panels generate to their local utility. According to writer Daniel H. Pink of *Wired* magazine, homeowners with solar panels are "operating as mini-utilities, selling excess electricity back to the power company."[6]

New technology also promises to make solar energy more attractive. A major new area of interest is in harnessing solar energy to make hydrogen fuel. Many scientists and policy makers are touting hydrogen as the fuel of the future. Hydrogen is the most abundant element in the universe, and cars that run on it produce no pollution. Unfortunately, while hydrogen energy is clean and

Rows and rows of solar panels, pictured here in California, are a less-than-attractive feature of solar power.

renewable, energy is needed to free it. Today, most hydrogen is derived from fossil fuels, a process that produces greenhouse gases. However, if solar energy were used to separate water into oxygen and hydrogen, the hydrogen produced would be clean. As part of its plan to transition the United States to a hydrogen economy, in 2005 the U.S. Department of Energy awarded $10 million in research contracts to eight universities to develop cost-effective new ways to use solar energy to make hydrogen.

Whether or not energy insecurity and technological innovation will make solar energy competitive remains to be seen.

Despite the enthusiasm of many solar-power proponents, critics argue that spending money on solar technologies is a waste of resources. The debate over the viability of solar power will certainly continue, as will efforts to make solar energy the world's primary power source. Like the ancients who captured this energy to heat their homes and preserve food, solar scientists are intrigued by the possibility of capturing the sun's rays to improve human life.

Notes

1. John Carey, "What's Raining on Solar's Parade?" *Business Week*, February 6, 2006, p. 78.

2. David Manners, "Solar Power Has the Wind in Its Sails," *Electronics Weekly*, February 8, 2006, p. 3.

3. Kwabena Osei, "Solar Energy: Africa's Second Liberation," *New Africa*, July 1, 2003, p. 40.

4. Quoted in Kristin Kellogg, "Solar Car Team Sees Limited Use for Public," *Missourian News*, July 13, 2005, p. B2.

5. Howard C. Hayden, *The Solar Fraud: Why Solar Energy Won't Run the World*, 2nd ed. Pueblo West, CO: Vales Lake, 2004, p. 1.

6. Daniel H. Pink, "The New Power Generation," *Wired*, May 2005. www.wired.com/wired/archive/13.05/solar.html.

For centuries people have attempted to harness the sun's energy. Pictured is a solar power machine from 1925.

CHAPTER 1

The Development of Solar Power

A Brief History of Solar Energy

Lucy Cogan

In the following selection Lucy Cogan presents a brief history of the use of solar energy from ancient to modern times. The Greeks were the first to record a use of solar power, Cogan states. Facing a shortage of home-heating fuel, they learned how to build houses with south-facing walls to take advantage of the passive warming provided by sunshine. Other early cultures, ranging from the Chinese to the Anasazi, also made use of solar energy, she explains. In the nineteenth century the first steps toward solar generation of electricity were taken. French physicist Edmond Becquerel discovered that certain materials would produce electricity when they were exposed to sunlight. This discovery of the photovoltaic (PV) effect led other scientists to develop PV cells that could convert sunlight to electricity more efficiently. Cogan is a student at Annesley College in South Australia.

The Greeks and Romans used solar energy to heat buildings and water. Greeks made use of the solar energy for growing vegetables in greenhouses. Many other early civilizations such as the Chinese, Anasazi and Pueblo used solar energy for heating like the Greeks and Romans. . . .

The Greeks were the first people to use solar energy to warm buildings. They found that by constructing their homes and buildings in a certain way they could make use of the sun during winter. While it may have been difficult for these ancient

Lucy Cogan, "History of Solar Cells & Solar Energy," *Annesley College, www.annesley. sa.edu.au.* Reproduced by permission.

people to understand solar energy, entire cities [were] built this way in 400 B.C.

The Greeks and Romans Use Passive Solar Heating

The Greeks wrote the first account of solar energy in the fourth century B.C. when low fuel supplies from the Middle East occurred. They discovered the best way to get the sunlight was to face the main rooms south while the north side of the buildings would be shielded from cold winds. They added eaves to the roof [to provide] shade for the southern windows in summer. In 212 B.C. Archimedes allegedly used solar energy to reduce the Roman navy (which was attacking Syracuse) to ashes by having soldiers reflect sunlight off their shields toward Roman sails.

The Romans used sun [light] for central heating and to heat water in their large central baths quickly, as the burning of wood was consuming forests around Rome. The Greeks discovered

Sunlight reflects off glass and sets fire to a ship in this seventeenth-century painting.

and introduced glass in the first century A.D. Dark coloured pottery was used to store goods and therefore increase thermal energy. The Romans and Greeks built houses run by solar energy and even built a glasshouse to grow cucumbers for Tiberius Caesar [Roman emperor, 31 B.C.–A.D. 14]. The Romans depended on sunlight more than the Greeks as solar energy was used to allow the Romans to enjoy the fruits and vegetables they brought back from the Middle East or Africa. The Romans were able to grow a variety of fruit and vegetables by controlling the climate by either covering the glass houses or leaving them open to the sun.

Other early civilizations such as the Chinese, Anasazi and Pueblo used solar energy for heating, water evaporation, and many other functions.

Making Electricity from Light

In 1839 French physicist Antoine-Cesar Becquerel observed that shining light on an electrode submerged in a conductive solution would create an electric current.

Also in 1839 a French physicist named Edmond Becquerel found that a certain material would produce a small amount of an electric current when it was exposed to a light. This was described as the photovoltaic (PV) effect. It was an interesting part of science for the next three quarters of a century. Afterwards, selenium PV cells were converting light to electricity at 1% to 2% efficiency. As a result, selenium was quickly adopted in the emerging field of photography for use in light-measuring devices.

In 1941, the American Russell Ohl invented a silicon solar cell. It is similar to a glass window, which allows the sunlight to come in a room, and traps the solar heat much like when a car is parked in the sunlight. There were steps toward using PV in the 1940s and early 1950s. Highly pure crystalline silicon was produced using [what is] called

In 1839 Antoine-Cesar Becquerel observed how light could be converted into an electric current.

the Czochralski process. In 1954, scientists at Bell Laboratories depended on the Czochralski process to develop the first crystalline silicon photovoltaic cell, which had an efficiency of 4%. In the second half of the 20th century, the science behind solar energy has been refined and the process has been more fully explained. As a result, the [reduced] cost of PV devices has put them into the

A scientist demonstrates how an old car gets its energy from a solar panel he installed in this photo from 1960.

mainstream of modern energy producers. This was caused in part by advances in the technology, where PV conversion efficiencies have improved considerably.

Improved solar cells became a good source of electricity for satellites. On earth, solar cells are mainly used when cheaper alternatives are unavailable. For example, it can be cheaper to use PV cells in remote locations where building long power lines is cost prohibitive. It is likely to be many years before solar energy will fully replace fossil fuels.

Scientists are still experimenting with solar cells to find the perfect solution. The Greeks and Romans started using solar energy, and one day hopefully most of the energy produced in the world will be from the sun.

How Solar Technology Developed in the Nineteenth Century

Charles Smith

In the following selection historian Charles Smith recounts
the innovations of nineteenth-century scientists that eventually led to modern solar technology. The effort to put solar
energy to work driving machines began in France, he states,
where in 1860 mathematics professor Auguste Mouchout
invented the first solar steam engine. In the 1870s British
bureaucrat William Adams took up where Mouchout left off
by constructing a solar steam engine heated by an array of
mirrors. Engineers Charles Tellier and John Ericsson further
refined solar technology at the end of the century.
Commercialization of solar technology was begun in 1900
by entrepreneur Aubrey Eneas. Smith is the director the
Sustainable Development Program at Appalachian State
University in North Carolina.

T he earliest known record of the direct conversion of solar
radiation into mechanical power belongs to Auguste
Mouchout, a mathematics instructor at the Lycee de Tours.
Mouchout began his solar work in 1860 after expressing grave
concerns about his country's dependence on coal. "It would be
prudent and wise not to fall asleep regarding this quasi-securi-
ty," he wrote. "Eventually industry will no longer find in Europe
the resources to satisfy its prodigious expansion. Coal will

Charles Smith, "Revisiting Solar Power's Past," *Technology Review*, Vol. 98, July,
1995, p. 38-47. © 1995 by the Association of Alumni and Alumnae of MIT.
Reproduced by permission.

undoubtedly be used up. What will industry do then?" By the following year he was granted the first patent for a motor running on solar power and continued to improve his design until about 1880. During this period the inventor laid the foundation for our modern understanding of converting solar radiation into mechanical steam power.

Mouchout's Solar Motor

Mouchout's initial experiments involved a glass-enclosed iron cauldron: incoming solar radiation passed through the glass cover, and the trapped rays transmitted heat to the water. While this simple arrangement boiled water, it was of little practical value because the quantities and pressures of steam it produced were

A colorful painting depicts 1860s France, where Auguste Mouchout invented the first solar-powered steam engine.

minimal. However, Mouchout soon discovered that by adding a reflector to concentrate additional radiation onto the cauldron, he could generate more steam. In late 1865, he succeeded in using his apparatus to operate a small, conventional steam engine.

By the following summer, Mouchout displayed his solar motor to Emperor Napoleon III in Paris. The monarch, favorably impressed, offered financial assistance for developing an industrial solar motor for France. With the newly acquired funds, Mouchout enlarged his invention's capacity, refined the reflector, redesigning it as a truncated cone, like a dish with slanted sides, to more accurately focus the sun's rays on the boiler. Mouchout also constructed a tracking mechanism that enabled the entire machine to follow the sun's altitude and azimuth, providing uninterrupted solar reception.

After six years of work, Mouchout exhibited his new machine in the library courtyard of his Tours home in 1872, amazing spectators. One reporter described the reflector as an inverted "mammoth lamp shade . . . coated on the inside with very thin silver leaf" and the boiler sitting in the middle as an "enormous thimble" made of blackened copper and "covered with a glass bell."

Anxious to put his invention to work, he connected the apparatus to a steam engine that powered a water pump. On what was deemed "an exceptionally hot day," the solar motor produced one-half horsepower. Mouchout reported the results and findings to the French Academy of Science. . . .

Adams Utilizes Mirrors for Further Innovations

During the height of Mouchout's experimentation, William Adams, the deputy registrar for the English Crown in Bombay, India, wrote an award-winning book entitled *Solar Heat: A Substitute for Fuel in Tropical Countries*. Adams noted that he was intrigued with Mouchout's solar steam engine after reading an account of the Tours demonstration, but that the invention was impractical, since "it would be impossible to construct [a dish-shaped reflector] of much greater dimensions" to generate more than Mouchout's one-half horsepower. The problem, he felt, was that the polished metal reflector would tarnish too easily, and

Emperor Napoleon III (pictured) helped fund the development of a solar motor for France after seeing Mouchout's successful experiments.

would be too costly to build and too unwieldy to efficiently track the sun.

Fortunately for the infant solar discipline, the English registrar did not spend all his time finding faults in the French inventor's efforts, but offered some creative solutions. For example, Adams was convinced that a reflector of flat silvered mirrors arranged in a semicircle would be cheaper to construct and easier to maintain. His plan was to build a large rack of many small mirrors and adjust each one to reflect sunlight in a specific direction. To track the sun's movement, the entire rack could be rolled around a semicircular track, projecting the concentrated radiation onto a stationary boiler. The rack could be attended by a laborer and would have to be moved only "three or four times during the day," Adams noted, or more frequently to improve performance.

Confident of his innovative arrangement, Adams began construction in late 1878. By gradually adding 17-by-10-inch flat mirrors and measuring the rising temperatures, he calculated that to generate the 1,200 [degrees] F [Fahrenheit] necessary to produce steam pressures high enough to operate conventional engines, the reflector would require 72 mirrors. To demonstrate the power of the concentrated radiation, Adams placed a piece of wood in the focus of the mirrored panes where, he noted, "it ignited immediately." He then arranged the collectors around a boiler, retaining Mouchout's enclosed cauldron configuration, and connected it to a 2.5-horsepower steam engine that operated during daylight hours "for a fortnight in the compound of [his] bungalow."

Eager to display his invention, Adams notified newspapers and invited his important friends—including the Army's commander in chief, a colonel from the Royal Engineers, the secretary of public works, various justices, and principal mill owners—to a demonstration. Adams wrote that all were impressed, even the local engineers who, while doubtful that solar power could compete directly with coal and wood, thought it could be a practical supplemental energy source. . . .

Tellier's Solar Pumps

Even with Mouchout's abandonment and the apparent disenchantment of England's sole participant, Europe continued to advance the practical application of solar heat, as the torch returned to France and engineer Charles Tellier. Considered by many the father of refrigeration, Tellier actually began his work in refrigeration as a result of his solar experimentation, which led to the design of the first nonconcentrating, or non-reflecting, solar motor.

In 1885, Tellier installed a solar collector on his roof similar to the flat-plate collectors placed atop many homes today for heating domestic water. The collector was composed of ten plates, each consisting of two iron sheets riveted together to form a watertight seal, and connected by tubes to form a single unit. Instead of filling the plates with water to produce steam, Tellier chose ammonia as a working fluid because of its significantly lower boiling point. After solar exposure, the containers emitted enough pressurized ammonia gas to power a water pump he had placed in his well at the rate of some 300 gallons per hour during daylight. Tellier considered his solar water pump practical for anyone with a south-facing roof. He also thought that simply adding plates, thereby increasing the size of the system, would make industrial applications possible.

By 1889 Tellier had increased the efficiency of the collectors by enclosing the top with glass and insulating the bottom. He published the results in *The Elevation of Water with the Solar Atmosphere*, which included details on his intentions to use the sun to manufacture ice. Like his countryman Mouchout, Tellier envisioned that the large expanses of the African plains could become industrially and agriculturally productive through the implementation of solar power.

In *The Peaceful Conquest of West Africa*, Tellier argued that a consistent and readily available supply of energy would be required to power the machinery of industry before the French holdings in Africa could be properly developed. He also pointed out that even though the price of coal had fallen since Mouchout's experiments, fuel continued to be a significant expense in French operations in Africa. He therefore concluded that the construction costs of his low-temperature, non-concentrating solar motor were low enough to justify its implementation. He also noted that his machine was far less costly than Mouchout's device, with its dish-shaped reflector and complicated tracking mechanism. . . .

Ericsson Invents the Parabolic Trough

Though Swedish by birth, John Ericsson was one of the most influential and controversial U.S. engineers of the nineteenth century. While he spent his most productive years designing machines of war—his most celebrated accomplishment was the Civil War battleship the *Monitor*—he dedicated the last 20 years of his life largely to more peaceful pursuits such as solar power.

The Civil War battleship Monitor, *designed by John Ericsson, sails along the choppy waters of the Atlantic Ocean.*

This work was inspired by a fear shared by virtually all of his fellow solar inventors that coal supplies would someday end. In 1868 he wrote, "A couple of thousand years dropped in the ocean of time will completely exhaust the coal fields of Europe, unless, in the meantime, the heat of the sun be employed."

Thus by 1870 Ericsson had developed what he claimed to be the first solar-powered steam engine, dismissing Mouchout's machine as "a mere toy." In truth, Ericsson's first designs greatly resembled Mouchout's devices, employing a conical, dish-shaped reflector that concentrated solar radiation onto a boiler and a tracking mechanism that kept the reflector directed toward the sun.

Though unjustified in claiming his design original, Ericsson soon did invent a novel method for collecting solar rays—the parabolic trough. Unlike a true parabola, which focuses solar radiation onto a single, relatively small area, or focal point, like a satellite television dish, a parabolic trough is more akin to an oil drum cut in half length-wise that focuses solar rays in a line across the open side of the reflector.

This type of reflector offered many advantages over its circular (dish-shaped) counterparts: it was comparatively simple, less expensive to construct, and, unlike a circular reflector, had only to track the sun in a single direction (up and down, if lying horizontal, or east to west if standing on end), thus eliminating the need for complex tracking machinery. The downside was that the device's temperatures and efficiencies were not as high as with a dish-shaped reflector, since the configuration spread radiation over a wider area—a line rather than a point. Still when Ericsson constructed a single linear boiler (essentially a pipe), placed it in the focus of the trough, positioned the new arrangement toward the sun, and connected it to a conventional steam engine, he claimed the machine ran successfully, though he declined to provide power ratings.

The new collection system became popular with later experimenters and eventually became a standard for modern plants. In fact, the largest solar systems in the last decade have opted for Ericsson's parabolic trough reflector because it strikes a good engineering compromise between efficiency and ease of operation.

For the next decade, Ericsson continued to refine his invention, trying lighter materials for the reflector and simplifying its construction. By 1888, he was so confident of his design's practical performance that he planned to mass-produce and supply the apparatus to the "owners of the sunburnt lands on the Pacific coast" for agricultural irrigation.

Unfortunately for the struggling discipline, Ericsson died the following year. And because he was a suspicious and, some said, paranoid man who kept his designs to himself until he filed patent applications, the detailed plans for his improved sun motor died with him. Nevertheless, the search for a practical solar motor was not abandoned. In fact, the experimentation and development of large-scale solar technology was just beginning.

Eneas Starts the First Solar Commercial Venture

Boston resident Aubrey Eneas began his solar motor experimentation in 1892, formed the first solar power company (The

Solar Motor Co.) in 1900, and continued his work until 1905. One of his first efforts resulted in a reflector much like Ericsson's early parabolic trough. But Eneas found that it could not attain sufficiently high temperatures, and, unable to unlock his predecessor's secrets, decided to scrap the concept altogether and return to Mouchout's truncated-cone reflector. Unfortunately, while Mouchout's approach resulted in higher temperatures, Eneas was still dissatisfied with the machine's performance. His solution was to make the bottom of the reflector's truncated cone-shaped dish larger by designing its sides to be more upright to focus radiation onto a boiler that was 50 percent larger.

Finally satisfied with the results, he decided to advertise his design by exhibiting it in sunny Pasadena, Calif., at Edwin Cawston's ostrich farm, a popular tourist attraction. The monstrous machine did not fail to attract attention. Its reflector, which spanned 33 feet in diameter, contained 1,788 individual mirrors. And its boiler, which was about 13 feet in length and a foot wide, held 100 gallons of water. After exposure to the sun, Eneas's device boiled the water and transferred steam through a flexible pipe to an engine that pumped 1,400 gallons of water per minute from a well onto the arid California landscape. . . .

The future, like the machine itself, looked bright and shiny.

Discovering How to Turn the Sun's Rays into Electricity

John Perlin

The most promising use of solar power for meeting the world's energy needs on a large scale requires turning the sun's rays into electricity. In the following selection John Perlin describes how the technology for making this conversion came about. In 1876, Perlin writes, researchers discovered that sunlight can induce an electrical current in selenium. The current was very weak, however; scientists eventually discovered in 1953 that silicon was a better material to use in photovoltaic cells. The first application of the cells was in satellites orbiting Earth. For other purposes, solar cells remained far too expensive to compete with other forms of electrical generation. This changed in the 1970s, when photovoltaic cells began to be installed in locations too remote to be connected by costly power lines to the electrical grid. Today, many rural areas continue to rely on solar cells for power. Perlin, of the California Solar Center, is a historian and author of several books, including *From Space to Earth— The Story of Solar Electricity*.

When [nineteenth-century British scientist] William Grylls Adams and his student, Richard Evans Day, discovered [in 1876] that an electrical current could be started in selenium solely by exposing it to light, they felt confident that they had dis-

John Perlin, "Solar Evolution: The History of Solar Energy," www.californiasolar center.org, 2005. Reproduced by permission. Also appearing in the forthcoming new edition of *A Golden Thread: 2500 Years of Solar Architecture and Technology*, by John Perlin and Ken Butti.

covered something completely new. [German electrical engineer] Werner von Siemens, a contemporary whose reputation in the field of electricity ranked him alongside Thomas Edison, called the discovery "scientifically of the most far-reaching importance." This pioneering work portended quantum mechanics long before most chemists and physicist[s] had accepted the reality of atoms. Although selenium solar cells failed to convert enough sunlight to power electrical equipment, they proved that a solid material could change light into electricity without heat or without moving parts.

In spring 1953, while researching silicon for its possible applications in electronics, Gerald Pearson, an empirical physicist at Bell Laboratories, inadvertently made a solar cell that was far more efficient than solar cells made from selenium. Two other Bell scientists—Daryl Chapin and Calvin Fuller—refined Pearson's discovery [and] came up with the first solar cell capable of converting enough of the sun's energy into power to run everyday electrical equipment. Reporting the Bell discovery, *The New York Times* praised it as "the beginning of a new era, leading eventually to the realization of harnessing the almost limitless energy of the sun for the uses of civilization."

The Solar Cell Was too Expensive

During the first years after the discovery of the silicon solar cell, its prohibitive cost kept it out of the electrical power market. Desperate to find commercial outlets for solar cells, novelty items such as toys and radios run by solar cells were manufactured and sold as this advertisement illustrates.

Although technical progress of silicon solar cells continued at breakneck speed—doubling their efficiency in eighteen months—commercial success eluded the Bell solar cell. A one-watt cell cost almost $300 per watt in 1956 while a commercial power plant cost 50 cents a watt to build at that time. The only demand for silicon solar cells came from radio and toy manufacturers to power miniature ships in wading pools, propellers of model DC-4's, and beach radios. With solar cells running only playthings, Daryl Chapin could not help but wonder, "What to do with our new baby?"

How a Photovoltaic Cell Works

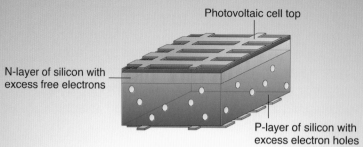

Photovoltaic cell top

N-layer of silicon with
excess free electrons

P-layer of silicon with
excess electron holes

Step 1

In a typical photovoltaic cell, two layers of silicon semiconductor are tightly bound
together. The N-layer has been modified to have excess free electrons, while the
P-layer has been modified to have excess electron holes.

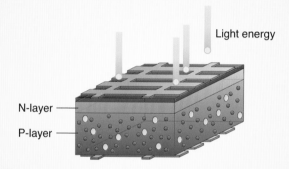

Light energy

N-layer

P-layer

Step 2

When sunlight strikes the cell, electrons are freed to travel randomly. Electrons
close to the boundary between the layers cross from one layer to the other but
cannot return in the same direction, creating a charge imbalance in each layer.
For example, when excess electrons move to the N-layer, the excess electrons
will try to leave the layer to correct the imbalance but cannot.

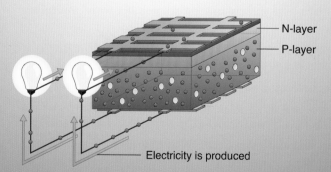

N-layer

P-layer

Electricity is produced

Step 3

Providing an external circuit along which the electrons can return naturally to the
P-layer produces an electric current.

Source: Matthew J. Parry-Hill, Robert T. Sutter, and Michael W. Davidson, National High Magnetic Field Laboratory,
Florida State University. http://micro.magnet.fus.edu.

While efforts to commercialize the silicon solar cell faltered, the Army and Air Force saw the device as the ideal power source for a top-secret project—earth-orbiting satellites. But when the Navy was awarded the task of launching America's first satellite, it rejected solar cells as an untried technology and decided to use chemical batteries as the power source for its Vanguard satellite. The late Dr. Hans Ziegler, probably the world's foremost expert in satellite instrumentation in the late 1950s, strongly differed with the Navy. He argued that conventional batteries would run out of power in days, silencing millions of dollars worth of electronic equipment. In contrast, solar cells could power a satellite for years. Through an unrelenting crusade led by Dr. Ziegler to get the Navy to change its mind, the Navy finally relented and as a compromise, put a dual power system of chemical batteries and silicon solar cells on the Vanguard. Just as Ziegler predicted, the batteries failed after a week or so, but the silicon solar cells kept the Vanguard communicating with Earth for years.

ANOTHER OPINION ➤

The Sun Can Meet All Humanity's Energy Needs

There's ten thousand times more solar power than we need for all our energy. The idea is to cover some fraction of the Earth with solar cells, and use those to convert optical power into, let's say, electricity.

Ted Sargent, "Nanoscience Guru Shares Large Visions of Tiny Tech's Future," *Kazinform*, March 1, 2006. www.inform.kz.

Solar Cells in Space

Despite solar cells' success in powering both American and Soviet satellites during the 1950s and early 1960s, many at NASA [National Aeronautics and Space Administration] doubted the technology's ability to power its more ambitious space ventures. The agency viewed solar cells as merely a stopgap measure until nuclear power systems became available. But solar engineers proved the skeptics wrong. They met the increasing power demands by designing ever larger and more powerful solar cell arrays. Nuclear energy, in contrast, never powered more than a handful of satellites. Hence, since the late 1960s, solar cells have become the accepted power source for the world's satellites.

The increasing demand for solar cells in space opened an increasing and relatively large business for those manufacturing solar cells. Even more significantly, our past, present and future application of space would have been impossible if not for solar cells. The telecommunication revolution would never have gotten off the ground if not for solar powered satellites. . . .

Solar-cell technology proved too expensive for terrestrial use until the early 1970s when Dr. Elliot Berman, with financial help from Exxon Corporation, designed a significantly less costly solar cell by using a poorer grade of silicon and packaging the cells with cheaper materials. Bringing the price down from $100 a watt to $20 per watt, [Berman-made] solar cells could now compete in situations where people needed electricity distant from power lines. Off-shore oil rigs, for example, required warning lights and horns to prevent ships from running into them but had no power other than toxic, cumbersome, short-lived batteries. Compared to their installation, maintenance and replacement, solar modules proved a bargain. Many gas and oil fields on land but far away from power lines needed small amounts of electricity to combat corrosion in well heads and piping. Once again, electricity from the sun saved the day. Major purchases of solar modules by the gas and oil industry gave the fledgling terrestrial solar cell industry the needed capital to persevere.

The Coast Guard Begins Using Solar Power

It cost the Coast Guard more money to install, maintain and replace the non rechargeable batteries that powered its buoys than the buoys themselves. A brave Coast Guard officer, then Lieutenant Commander Lloyd Lomer, who had training in optics and physics, believed that their replacement by solar modules could save taxpayers millions of dollars and do the job better. But his commander refused to listen. Exasperated by such stonewalling, Lomer finally appealed to higher authorities and got the nod to solarize the Coast Guard's navigational aids [in the 1980s]. President Ronald Reagan commended Lomer for "saving a substantial amount of the taxpayers' money through your initiative and managerial effectiveness as project manager for the conversion of aids to navigation from battery to solar photovoltaic power." Thanks to Lomer's persistence, not only does the U.S. Coast Guard rely almost entirely on solar power for all of its buoys and light houses but so do all the other Coast Guards throughout the world. . . .

Solar arrays, such as these at the top of this space station, provide power for various spacecraft.

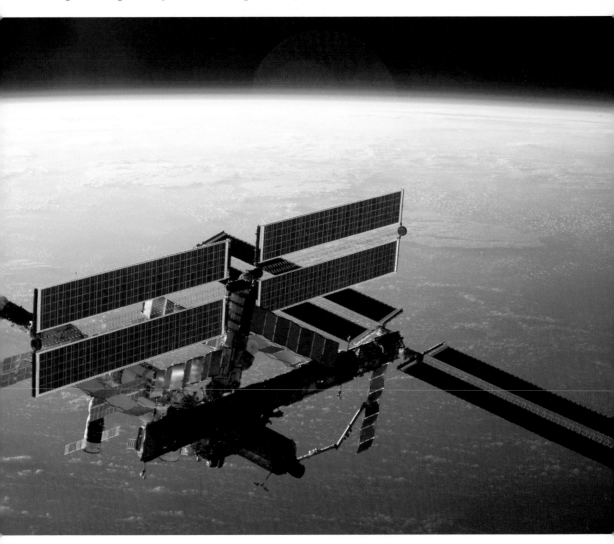

Though it lacks running water or any other conveniences of modern life, this shack in Baja, Mexico, has electricity thanks to a solar panel (right).

Solar Power Grows in Rural Areas

From the 1960s through the 1980s, experts planned to power rural parts of the developing world—where the majority live—according to the Western model: build centralized generating plants and by networks of wires transmit the electricity to consumers. But constructing such networks has proven too costly, leaving billions of rural people without electricity. These people have had to rely on costly and inadequate ad hoc solutions to light their homes and power their appliances such as kerosene lamps, automobile batteries and generators. In many cases, solar cells have provided to those living far away from electrical lines the means to obtain higher quality lighting and more reliable power. Since 1983, half of the households in the outlying islands of Tahiti have relied on solar-generated power. More rural Kenyans use electricity from the sun than that offered by the national utility. At least one hundred thousand families in Mexico, Central America and the West Indies run their lights, television sets, and radios with solar electricity. These successes has led the World Energy Council, the international organization of utilities, to recognize, "Solar cells for use at individual houses are a very important development that warrants particular attention as they are ideal for low-power rural applications." . . .

The solar-cell industry has grown dramatically over the last twenty years, increasing output 200 fold in this time period. Today, those needing power in remote areas no longer regard solar cells as an alternative source of energy but consider them the most effective solution. Institutions like the World Bank now believe that solar cells "have an important and growing part to play in providing electrical services to the developing world." In less developed countries, where over half of the population must travel over two hours just to make a phone call, the United Nations today sees solar cells offering these people "for the first time a real practical possibility of reliable telecommunications for general use."

How Today's Solar Technology Works

Union of Concerned Scientists

In the selection that follows, the Union of Concerned Scientists (UCS) explains the various ways that solar energy is used. Some uses are passive, the UCS points out, as when sunlight is allowed in through a window to light rooms within a building. If deliberately designed to exploit the sun's energy, a passive solar home can absorb solar heat in the winter and deflect it the summer, the organization explains. Additionally, buildings can be outfitted with solar collectors, which sit on rooftops gathering sunlight and converting it to heat for use inside. Solar concentrators use reflectors to focus the sun's rays on a small surface, heating it. This heat can be used to turn water into steam, which in turn can drive a generator to produce electricity. The most recent of solar technologies is the photovoltaic cell. The UCS explains that a photovoltaic cell takes advantage of the tendency of electrons to shake loose from silicon atoms when struck by sunlight. The loose electrons are then channeled into an electrical current. The Union of Concerned Scientists is a nonprofit alliance of more than one-hundred thousand concerned citizens and scientists committed to a cleaner, healthier environment and a safer world.

Solar energy, power from the sun, is free and inexhaustible. In the broadest sense, solar energy supports all life on earth and is the basis for almost every form of energy we use. . . .

Union of Concerned Scientists, "How Solar Energy Works," *ucsusa.org*, September 19, 2005. Reproduced by permission.

The amount of energy from the sun that falls on the earth is enormous. All the energy stored in the earth's reserves of coal, oil, and natural gas is matched by the energy from 20 days of sunshine. Outside the earth's atmosphere, the sun's energy contains about 1,300 watts per square meter. About one-third of this light is reflected back into space, and some is absorbed by the atmosphere (in part causing winds to blow).

Passive and Active Solar Housing

Passive Solar House

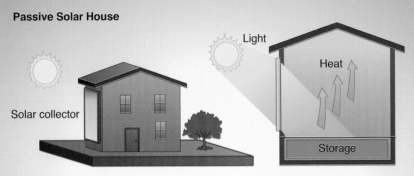

Passive solar homes are designed to use incoming sunlight effectively. They feature quality insulation and are positioned to let maximum amounts of light in.

Active Solar House

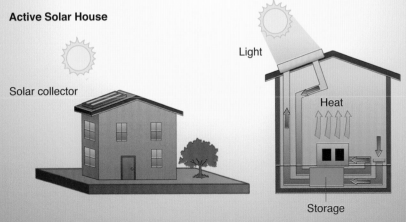

Active solar houses use technology to collect and store energy for space and water heating.

Source: U.S. Department of Energy.

Three Types of Solar Power

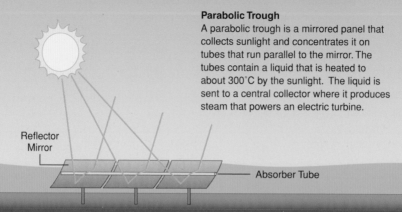

Parabolic Trough

A parabolic trough is a mirrored panel that collects sunlight and concentrates it on tubes that run parallel to the mirror. The tubes contain a liquid that is heated to about 300˚C by the sunlight. The liquid is sent to a central collector where it produces steam that powers an electric turbine.

Reflector Mirror

Absorber Tube

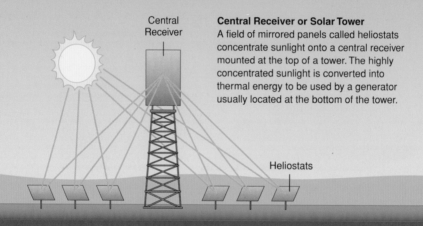

Central Receiver

Central Receiver or Solar Tower

A field of mirrored panels called heliostats concentrate sunlight onto a central receiver mounted at the top of a tower. The highly concentrated sunlight is converted into thermal energy to be used by a generator usually located at the bottom of the tower.

Heliostats

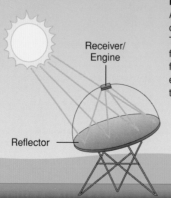

Receiver/ Engine

Parabolic Dish

A parabolic dish concentrates sunlight onto a single point in the center of the dish. This receiver uses the sunlight to heat a fluid or gas to approximately 750˚C. This fluid or gas is then used to generate electricity in a small engine or a micro turbine, attached to the receiver.

Reflector

Source: U.S. Department of Energy, Office of Energy Efficiency and Renewable Energy. www.eere.doe.gov.

By the time it reaches the earth's surface, the energy in sunlight has fallen to about 1,000 watts per square meter, at noon on a cloudless day. Averaged over the entire surface of the earth, 24 hours per day for a year, each square meter collects about the energy a equivalent of a barrel of oil. . . .

Solar Design for Buildings

One simple, obvious use of sunlight is to light our buildings. If properly designed, buildings can capture the sun's heat in the winter and avoid it in the summer, while using daylight year round. Buildings designed with the sun in mind can be comfortable and beautiful places to live and work.

Residential and commercial buildings account for one-third of U.S. energy use, including the energy used to make the electricity used in buildings. Solar design, better insulation, and more efficient appliances could reduce this demand by 60 to 80 percent. There are more than 250,000 passive solar homes in America, but there should be many more. Simple design features, such as properly orienting a house toward the south, putting most windows on the south side of the building, and allowing for cooling breezes in the summer, are inexpensive yet improve the comfort and efficiency of a home.

Solar Heat Collectors

Besides using design features to maximize use of the sun, some buildings have active systems to gather and store solar energy. Solar collectors sit on the rooftops of buildings to collect solar energy for space heating, water heating, and space cooling. Most solar collector are large flat boxes, painted black on the inside, with glass covers. In the most common design, pipes in the box carry liquids that take the heat from the box and bring it into the building. This heated liquid, usually a water-alcohol mixture to prevent freezing, is used to heat water in a tank or is put through radiators to heat the air. . . .

Solar collectors were very popular in the early 1980s, in the aftermath of the energy crisis. Federal tax credits for residential solar collectors also helped. In 1984, 16 million square feet of collectors were sold in the United States. When fossil fuel prices dropped in the mid-1980s, and President Reagan did away with the tax credit in 1985, demand for solar collectors plummeted. . . .

Solar Thermal Concentrators

By using mirrors and lenses to concentrate the rays of the sun, solar thermal systems can produce very high temperatures, as high as 3,000 degrees C [centigrade]. This intense heat can be used in industrial applications, like boiling water to sterilize soup cans or to produce electricity.

Solar concentrators come in three main designs, parabolic troughs, parabolic dishes and central receivers. The most common is parabolic troughs, long curved mirrors that concentrate sunlight on a liquid inside a tube that runs parallel to the mirror. The liquid, at about 300 degrees C, runs to a central collector, where it produces steam that drives an electric turbine.

Parabolic dish concentrators are similar to trough concentrators, but focus the sunlight on a single point. Dishes can produce much higher temperatures, and so can produce electricity more efficiently. But because they are more complicated, they have not succeeded outside of demonstration projects. . . .

The third type of concentrator system is a central receiver. One plant in California is a "power tower" design. A 17-acre field of mirrors concentrates sunlight on the top of an 80-meter-tall tower. The intense heat boils water instantly into steam, which drives a 10-megawatt generator at the base of the tower. Operated from 1982 to 1988, Solar One had a number of problems. It is now being restored and improved as Solar Two.

Photovoltaics

In 1839, French scientist Edmund Becquerel discovered that certain materials would give off a spark of electricity when struck with sunlight. This "photoelectric" effect was used in primitive solar cells made of selenium in the late 1800s. The first solar cells were used as light meters for photography. In the 1950s, scientists at Bell Labs revisited the technology, and, using silicon, produced solar cells that could convert 4 percent of the energy in sunlight directly to electricity. Within a few years, these panels were powering spaceships and satellites.

A solar-powered car races down the road in Australia's World Solar Car Challenge in 2001.

Solar cells work because the silicon used has a weak grip on its electrons. Cells are made of two layers of silicon, one with too many electrons (the n-layer) and one with too few (the p-layer). When light hits the first layer, electrons are knocked loose. As they flow toward the layer with too few electrons, they pass through an electric circuit, powering equipment. . . .

While many solar panels are used for off-grid homes, they are also used for powering cellular phone transmitters, road signs, water pumps, and millions of solar watches and calculators. Experimental solar-powered cars have raced across Australia. Still, most of the market is concentrated in off-grid homes, in the villages of developing countries and the vacation homes of industrial countries. Developing nations see PV as a way to avoid building long and expensive power lines to remote areas. . . .

As the cost of photovoltaics continues to decline, they will find increasingly larger niches. No other electrical generator is as easy to install or maintain. Even among renewables, PV has great potential. Made of silicon, one of the most plentiful materials on earth, and drawing power from the everlasting sun, they will never run into problems of scarcity. As prices continue to fall, solar power will become a significant source of electricity in the 21st century.

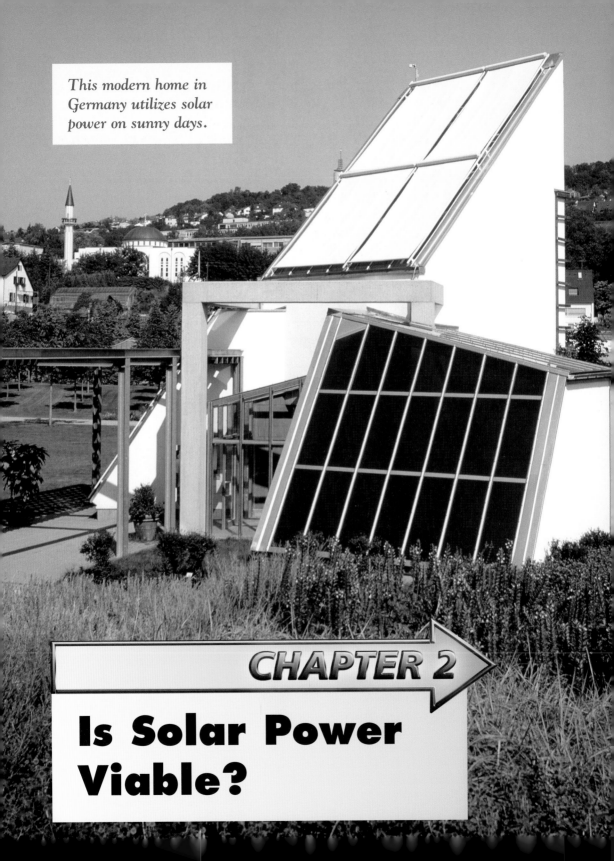

This modern home in Germany utilizes solar power on sunny days.

CHAPTER 2

Is Solar Power Viable?

Solar Power Can Make America Energy Independent

Liz Borkowski

Transitioning to solar power could reduce global warming caused by fossil fuel use, argues Liz Borkowski in the following selection. Solar power can also free the United States from its dependence on foreign sources of oil, she declares. One of the reasons solar power is so promising, Borkowski argues, is that it is practical for electrical generation just about everywhere that sunlight reaches the earth. Japan has shown that with a substantial investment in solar energy, the price of electricity generated by the sun can compete with that generated by fossil fuels, she claims. Borkowski is managing editor of *Co-op America Quarterly*.

If we want our children and grandchildren to inherit the clean renewable-energy future rather than the catastrophic climate-change future, we must act now to reverse the current trend of increasing atmospheric concentration of carbon dioxide (CO_2). This will require reducing our use of fossil fuels, which release greenhouse gases when they're burned for energy. Gradually shifting toward more efficient technologies and renewable energy sources won't be enough—we must catalyze a massive shift in our energy use within the next decade to stabilize our climate while meeting the world's growing power needs. Since our country accounts for more than 20 percent of world

Liz Borkowski, "The Promise of the Solar Future," *Co-op America Quarterly*, Summer, 2005, p. 9–11. © 2005 Co-op America. All rights reserved. Reproduced by permission.

greenhouse gas emissions, it is particularly important that we in the US lead the way.

The good news is that we have the knowledge, technology, and capacity to make the shift to a renewable energy path—it all hinges on growing solar power.

Solar energy is essential to a renewable energy future. Even after we achieve all possible energy-efficiency gains and take full advantage of other renewable energy sources, such as wind and geothermal, we'll still need some other way to generate at least 30 percent of our power. (This gap between energy demand and renewable energy supply for all energy, not only electricity, could be as much as 70 percent without aggressive energy efficiency.) That remaining energy must come from solar, because the alternatives—more fossil-fuel or nuclear power sources—won't eliminate the dangers we're facing today.

Stopping global warming and all its terrible consequences is reason enough to invest in solar energy, but shifting to solar will also bring many other benefits that are even more immediate and noticeable. Replacing fossil-fuel power with clean, affordable solar power will curb pollution and global warming, which will in turn improve our health and economic picture. At the same time, relying more on solar power and less on fossil fuels and nuclear energy will make us safer and more secure.

Freedom from Oil

With solar power, our country can become energy independent. Once we no longer rely on oil, our economy won't be vulnerable to supply disruptions in oil-producing countries, and no one will need to worry that our foreign policy might be influenced by our need to import oil from other parts of the world. As we phase out nuclear power, we'll have less need to fear accidents or sabotage that could expose millions of people to deadly radiation. Also, solar power production doesn't need to be centralized the way most of our electricity production is; with smaller power networks, we're much less likely to see large-scale blackouts like the one that hit the Northeast in the summer of 2003, and energy systems will present fewer appealing targets for would-be saboteurs. The whole system will be less expensive and more efficient—requiring less investment in expensive, often-protested

Solar Power: Looking into the Future

By 2025, solar energy is expected to thrive:

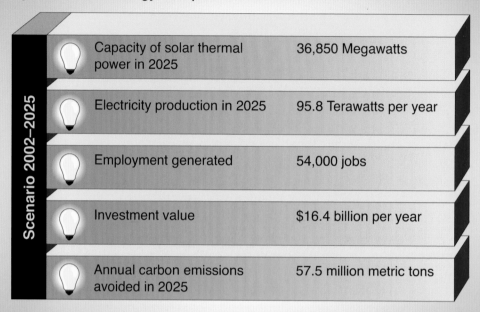

Scenario 2002–2025		
Capacity of solar thermal power in 2025	36,850 Megawatts
Electricity production in 2025	95.8 Terawatts per year
Employment generated	54,000 jobs
Investment value	$16.4 billion per year
Annual carbon emissions avoided in 2025	57.5 million metric tons

Source: U.S. Department of Energy, Office of Energy Efficiency and Renewable Energy. www.eere.doe.gov.

long-distance transmission lines, and avoiding transmission losses (up to 20 percent) of moving electricity long distance. Finally, with less pollution coming from fossil-fuel sources, the rates of asthma and other respiratory illnesses—which are currently on the rise, especially among urban children—will drop, bringing us lower health care costs and increased productivity.

Why are we so excited about solar power in particular? Staving off climate change requires immediate, dramatic action, and the solar energy sector is poised right now for just such a leap. If we take immediate action, solar energy could soon be competitive with coal-fired power. Within the next two decades, and possibly within five to ten years, the price of solar could drop to one-sixth of its current level, and utilities could be replacing aging coal-fired plants with arrays of solar photovoltaic (PV) panels. Solar power comes from light, not heat, so solar is available just about anywhere and will work even in cloudy and rainy areas; a report by the Solar Energy Industries Association found that a typical home in Maine needs only 25 percent more roof space than a home in sunny Los Angeles to meet its electricity needs from solar. And as solar power comes down in price, solar can provide the energy for heating, industrial uses, and transportation by creating the hydrogen for fuel cells or the energy for high-efficiency batteries. The cost of solar in Japan has dropped by 70 percent, so solar is now competitive with the cost of electricity for Japanese consumers. In short, solar can replace dirty power sources anywhere in our country—and be pumping out clean, reliable, affordable energy within the next decade.

Of course, a renewable-energy future will build on all existing renewable-energy technologies, including wind power, geothermal energy, and small-scale hydropower, and will require improvements in energy efficiency. We cannot have a renewable energy future without solar, though, so we must act now to make it affordable and available across the country and around the world. . . .

The Solar Future

If we act quickly to make the US solar PV industry competitive, we can share in some of the wealth that's currently moving to European countries and Japan to meet those nations' increased demand for renewable-energy sources. A great deal of innovation is due to occur within this industry as companies invest in large-scale manufacturing facilities; make breakthrough

advances in silicon, thin-film, and nano-based technologies; and streamline the packaging and installation of solar for different applications. Under the SHINE [Solar High-Impact National Energy] plan, more than 580,000 well-paying US jobs will be created. Even if we miss the opportunity to keep PV manufacturing in the US, every state in the nation will be able to create PV-installation jobs that can't be shipped overseas.

If the US adopts SHINE, the rest of the world will also benefit. Given our country's disproportionate contributions to global-warming emissions, our actions will play a major role in determining the severity of the climate-change impacts on our planet. Also, if our increased demand for solar spurs improvement in PV's efficiency and affordability, that will make it easier for the millions of people around the world who live without electricity to adopt solar systems. It's in our best interests to allow developing countries to "leapfrog" to renewable energy without first using fossil fuels on a large scale, because doing so will also help slow climate change.

David Austin. Reproduced by permission.

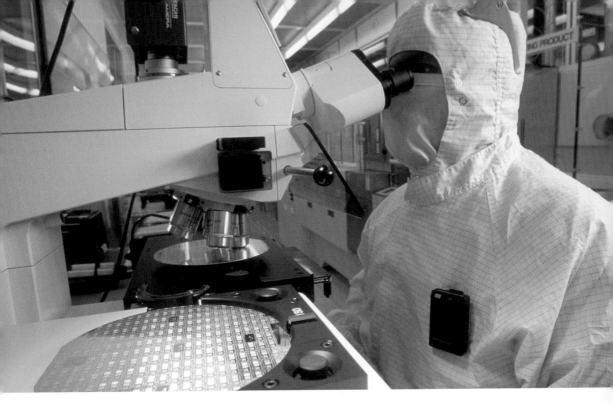

A worker tests silicon wafers at a semiconductor plant in Washington. Some feel it is necessary to make advances in technology to reduce America's dependence on oil.

Individuals, communities, cities, and states are taking steps to reduce their global-warming impacts by advancing energy efficiency and renewable-energy power sources. Any actions that your family takes—from installing rooftop solar panels to advocating for the use of solar energy in your community—will have the dual benefit of reducing your global-warming impacts while helping to demonstrate the viability of and growing support for solar power.

The choices we make now will determine what kind of world our children and grandchildren inherit from us. If we stay on our current path, theirs will be a world full of scarcity, natural disasters, and conflict. If we act quickly to create a renewable-energy future with solar as a key pillar, they can live in a cleaner environment and a safer, more prosperous world. Before this window of opportunity closes, we must commit to the goal of a clean energy future and act together to make this dream a reality.

The good news is that we can start the solar future today.

Solar Power Cannot Make America Energy Independent

Mike Oliver and John Hospers

> Relying on solar power to meet the nation's future energy needs is misguided, argue Mike Oliver and John Hospers in the selection that follows. Solar energy has some limited, small-scale applications, such as powering instruments in space, they claim, but using solar energy to generate electricity for urban areas is simply impractical. The central problem with solar power is that the sun's rays are too diffuse. Additionally, solar energy is intermittent, with little solar power reaching the ground on cloudy days and none at night. Collecting and concentrating solar energy has proven to be far too costly to be worthwhile, they contend. Also, the environmental consequences of a global effort to switch to solar power would be harmful, the authors claim. It would require large areas of land and consume huge quantities of raw materials, such as aluminum. Oliver is a physicist and engineer, now retired. Hospers, emeritus professor of philosophy at the University of Southern California, was the first candidate nominated by the Libertarian Party for the office of U.S. president.

Solar energy is useful for energizing the instruments on spacecraft not farther from the sun than Mars. On Earth it can be helpful in minor tasks such as heating water. But it is useless for

Mike Oliver and John Hospers, "Alternative Fuels?," *The American Enterprise*, Vol. 12, September 1, 2001, p. 20. Copyright 2001 American Enterprise Institute for Public Policy Research. Reproduced with permission of *The American Enterprise*, a national magazine of politics, business, and culture (taemag.com).

electrifying cities. The land and construction needs for solar generation are at least 500 times larger than those of fossil fuel or nuclear plants of equal capacity, while requiring far more upkeep and operating costs. This is why not even sunny Israel—or any other nation, anywhere—is using solar electricity except in meager trifles. . . .

The sun provides us with huge amounts of energy, but it comes at a small rate for any given area, so the sun is a low-grade energy source. This is more important than the fact that it is omnipresent, and large in total value.

Consider: There are untold millions of tons of gold in the earth's oceans. Why aren't we taking this gold from the seas? It is the dilution that stops us. If we can't obtain at least $8 worth of gold from a ton of water, we will go broke from the costs of extraction. Just as low-grade ore can be abundant yet uneconomic, bankrupting those foolish enough to go after it, many Americans have been misled into believing that low-grade energy can be a bonanza.

A Diluted Resource

You might not think of solar energy as low grade if you are in the Sahara, but even 130 degrees Fahrenheit doesn't compare to the heat in the cylinders of your car, which is 1,000 degrees or more. Wood, coal, oil, and gas may have derived their energy value from the sun, but the energy in them accumulated over long periods of time and their combustion can easily give us 1,000 degrees and even higher temperatures.

On a sunny cloudless day, solar energy comes to earth at a rate of one kilowatt per square meter per hour. This means that if there were no conversion losses for solar power plants, and if the sun shone a reliable eight hours a day throughout the U.S., we could tell the sheiks and ayatollahs where to go with their oil. But there is no energy transfer without loss, and the conversion losses for solar electric plants are, to put it mildly, extreme. As a result, huge areas must be covered with solar collectors to derive even a relatively low amount of useable electricity. This is true whether we use solar energy to produce heat which is converted into electricity, or photovoltaic cells for direct generation. In addition, solar rays are not available at night, and they are often obstructed by snow, dust, and clouds even during daytime. Batteries or stored heat offer a means of stockpiling solar electricity for use during nights or cloudy days—but this is expensive.

The former solar electric plant at Barstow, California illustrates the fiasco of solar electricity with facts and figures. It concentrated solar rays to produce sufficient heat to drive turbo-electric generators. The facility occupied 75 acres of land and contained 1,916 heliostats, each of which was equipped with a moveable platform and reflector, as well as motors and controllers to follow the sun. Accounting for nights, clouds, and equipment

Limited Uses for Solar Power

Number of solar collectors (in millions of square feet)

Pool heating	Water heating	All other
11.1	0.4	0.2

Aside from heating swimming pools, solar energy is minimally used to meet other heating needs.

Source: U.S. Department of Energy, Energy Information Administration, 2004. www.eia.doe.gov.

maintenance and breakdowns, these heliostats operated an average of only six hours a day.

In its top state, the plant had a capacity of 10 million watts. Yet on average it furnished merely 20 percent of that amount. At ten cents per kilowatt-hour, the plant's total energy output was thus worth only $1,752,000 per year, assuming it generated as much electricity in winter as in summer. Unfortunately, its 850,000 square feet of reflectors needed cleaning once a week, and labor costs on top of other operating, maintenance, and repair expenses, far exceeded the value of the electricity the plant produced. Moreover, the total construction costs for the facility came to a staggering $199,000,000. This means the plant grossed less than 1 percent per year of its cost. In the end, the companies and government agencies which subsidized this project lost so much money they had to shut the plant down.

Sky-High Costs

Putting the entire U.S. on a solar electric regimen would require an initial expenditure of at least $30 trillion, plus trillions more each year for upkeep and maintenance. Enthusiasts also overlook the fact that we would need more than 500 times as much construction material (copper, iron, concrete, steel, etc.) to build solar generators as would be required for conventional power plants. All of this would have to be mined, processed, and moved to the solar sites. To bring it there, millions of loaded trucks would roam the highways day and night for many decades. Entire mountain ranges would have to be ripped up to provide the staggering amount of gravel, asphalt, cement, metals, etc. required.

Also overlooked is the fact that the mass of receptors, motors, rotating platforms, and reflectors required for a national solar electric system would occupy some 25,000 square miles of land. Much of this would need paving to facilitate access for maintenance.

Few creatures could live amidst the jumble. And even more land would have to be continuously disturbed to provide resources for replacement parts to keep the system going.

And then there are the bulky solar devices themselves. Researchers Dixy Lee Ray and Lou Guzzo have totaled up the materials needed to build a solar electric plant with a capacity of 1 billion watts: 35,000 tons of aluminum; 2 million tons of concrete; 7,500 tons of copper; 600,000 tons of steel; 75,000 tons of glass; 1,500 tons of chromium and titanium.

These solar panels at a plant that closed in Barstow, California, are no longer in use.

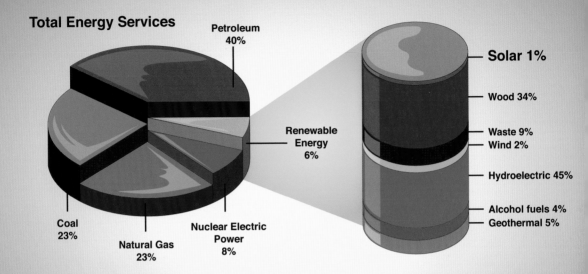

Solar Power Supplies a Fraction of America's Energy Needs

Total Energy Services

Petroleum 40%

Renewable Energy 6%

Coal 23%

Natural Gas 23%

Nuclear Electric Power 8%

Solar 1%

Wood 34%

Waste 9%
Wind 2%

Hydroelectric 45%

Alcohol fuels 4%
Geothermal 5%

Renewable energy supplies just 6 percent of America's energy, and solar power provides just 1 percent.

Source: U.S. Department of Energy, Energy Information Administration, 2004. www.eia.doe.gov.

An Inefficient Energy Source

Keep in mind that because fossil and nuclear plants operate at 65 to 89 percent of their maximum capacity on average, while solar electric plants output a mere 20 percent of their capacity on average (because of the intermittency of solar radiation), it would take a solar electric facility having a maximum capacity of at least 4 billion watts to replace a nuclear power plant with a maximum capacity of 1 billion watts. This is yet another point which environmentalists fail to mention when blithely promoting solar power.

Put these various facts together, and the picture is ugly: A solar plant capable of serving all the electricity needs of a modest city of 1 million people would use as much material as the paving of an interstate highway between Boston and Los Angeles. At least 400 square miles of land, filled solid with solar receptors, would be needed just to energize New York City—and this doesn't even consider the problem of clearing the snow off all that land during winter storms. The truth is, even in a sunny locale like Los Angeles, such a system wouldn't work, for its construction and maintenance costs would burden the citizenry with huge principal, interest, and operating costs.

It is easy to see why no nation on earth—none—has gone solar for significant electricity production. Indeed, in the U.S., all "alternative energy" sources put together provide us with less than 1 percent of our electric needs, despite government subsidies, grants from large foundations, and a barrage of media support.

Solar Power Can Benefit Rich Nations

Robert F. Service

Concerns about the rising cost of petroleum and the harmful impact of fossil fuels on the environment have revived interest in solar energy. In the following selection Robert F. Service reports that an increasing number of scientists think the United States should increase research into making solar power more efficient and economical. The sun can support developed nations' enormous demand for energy, but, Service points out, gathering and storing that energy remains expensive. A national effort along the lines of the *Apollo* moon-landing mission of the 1960s might make it possible to create new, cheaper solar technologies, he contends. Service is a correspondent for the journal *Science*.

Ask most Americans about their energy concerns, and you are likely to get an earful about gasoline prices. Ask Nate Lewis, and you'll hear about terawatts. Lewis, a chemist at the California Institute of Technology in Pasadena, is on a mission to get policymakers to face the need for sources of clean energy. He points out that humans today collectively consume the equivalent of a steady 13 terawatts (TW)—that's 13 trillion watts—of power. Eighty-five percent of that comes from fossil fuels that belch carbon dioxide, the primary greenhouse gas, into the atmosphere. Now, with CO_2 [carbon dioxide] levels at their highest point in 125,000 years, our planet is in the middle of a global experiment.

America's Solar Power Potential

The American Southwest could harness the most solar power—about 7 or 8 kilowatts per hour, per day.

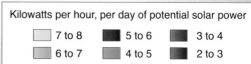

Kilowatts per hour, per day of potential solar power

- 7 to 8
- 6 to 7
- 5 to 6
- 4 to 5
- 3 to 4
- 2 to 3

Source: National Renewable Energy Laboratory. http://rredc.nrel.gov.

To slow the buildup of those gases, people will have to replace most, if not all, of those 13 TW with carbon-free energy sources. And that's the easy part. Thanks to global population growth and economic development, most energy experts predict we will need somewhere around an additional 30 TW by 2050. Coming up with that power in a way that doesn't trigger catastrophic changes in Earth's climate, Lewis says, "is unarguably the greatest technological challenge this country will face in the next 50 years."

Clearly, there are no easy answers. But one question Lewis and plenty of other high-profile scientists are asking is whether it's time to launch a major research initiative on solar energy. In April [2005], Lewis and physicist George Crabtree of Argonne National Laboratory in Illinois co-chaired a U.S. Department of Energy (DOE) workshop designed to explore the emerging potential for basic research in solar energy, from novel photovoltaics to systems for using sunlight to generate chemical fuels. Last week, the pair released their report on the Web (www.sc.doe.gov/bes/reports/list.html). . . .

The report outlines research priorities for improving solar power. It doesn't say how much money is needed to reach those goals, but DOE officials have floated funding numbers of about $50 million a year. That's up from the $10 million to $13 million a year now being spent on basic solar energy research. But given the scale of the challenge in transforming the energy landscape, other researchers and politicians are calling for far more.

Scientists Support Solar Energy

It is too early to say whether the money or the political support will fall in line. But it is clear that support for a renewed push for solar energy research is building among scientists. Last month [June 2005], Lewis previewed his upcoming report for members of DOE's Basic Energy Sciences Advisory Committee (BESAC), which regularly must weigh its support for facilities that include x-ray synchrotrons, neutron sources, nanoscience centers, and core research budgets. Despite a painfully lean budget outlook at DOE, support for a solar research program "is nearly unanimous," says Samuel Stupp, a BESAC member and chemist at Northwestern University in Evanston, Illinois.

Why? Terawatts. Even if a cheap, abundant, carbon-free energy source were to appear overnight, Lewis and others point out, it would still be a Herculean task to install the new systems fast enough just to keep up with rising energy demand—let alone to replace oil, natural gas, and coal. Generating 10 TW of energy—about 1/3 of the projected new demand by 2050—would require 10,000 nuclear power plants, each capable of churning out a gigawatt of power, enough to light a small city. "That means opening one nuclear reactor every other day for the next 50 years," Lewis says. Mind you, there hasn't been a new nuclear plant built in the United States since 1973, and concerns about high up-front capital costs, waste disposal, corporate liability, nuclear proliferation, and terrorism make it unlikely that will change in any meaningful way soon. . . .

So what is the world to do? Right now the solution is clear: The United States is currently opening natural gas plants at the rate of about one every 3.5 days. A stroll through Beijing makes it clear that China is pursuing coal just as fast. Fossil fuel use shows no signs of slowing.

Handwringing geologists have been warning for years that worldwide oil production is likely to peak sometime between now and 2040, driving oil prices through the roof. . . .

The Problems with Solar Energy

What's left? Solar. Photovoltaic panels currently turn sunlight into 3 gigawatts of electricity. The business is growing at 40% a year and is already a $7.5 billion industry. But impressive as it is, that's still a drop in the bucket of humanity's total energy use. "You have to use a logarithmic scale to see it" graphed next to fossil fuels, Lewis says.

What solar does have going for it is, well, the sun. Our star puts out 3.8 x 1023 kilowatt-hours of energy every hour. Of that, 170,000 TW strike Earth every moment, nearly one-third of which are reflected back into space. The bottom line is that every hour, Earth's surface receives more energy from the sun than humans use in a year.

Collecting even a tiny fraction of that energy won't be easy. To harvest 20 TW with solar panels that are 10% efficient at turning sunlight to electricity—a number well within the range of current technology—would require covering about 0.16% of Earth's land surface with solar panels. Covering all 70 million detached homes in the United States with solar panels would produce only 0.25 TW of electricity, just 1/10 of the electric power consumed in the country in the year 2000. That means land will need to be dedicated for solar farms, setting up land use battles that will likely raise environmental concerns, such as destroying habitat for species where the farms are sited.

Solar energy advocates acknowledge that a global solar energy grid would face plenty of other challenges as well. Chief among them: transporting and storing the energy. If massive solar farms are plunked down in the middle of deserts and other sparsely populated areas, governments will have to build an electrical infrastructure to transport the power to urban centers. That is certainly doable, but expensive.

High Costs

The issue of cost may be solar energy's biggest hurdle. Even without the extra infrastructure, harvesting power from the sun remains one of the most expensive renewable technologies on the market and far more expensive than the competition. In his . . . presentation last month [June 2005], Lewis noted that electricity derived from photovoltaics typically costs $0.25 to $0.50 per kilowatt-hour. By contrast, wind power costs $0.05 to $0.07, natural gas costs $0.025 to $0.05, and coal $0.01 to $0.04. What is more, electricity makes up only about 10% of the world's energy use. Globally, most energy goes toward heating homes, something that can usually be done more cheaply than with electricity generated from fossil fuels. . . .

Fiore. Reproduced by permission.

A researcher cleans mirrors on experimental solar reflectors.

In the wake of the oil shocks of the 1970s, the Carter Administration directed billions of dollars to alternative energy research. The big differences now are the threat of climate change and the current huge budget deficits in the United States. Some of the cost numbers have changed, but the gap between solar energy's potential and what is needed for it to be practical on a massive scale remains wide. The April [2005] DOE meeting explored many ideas to bridge that gap, including creating plastic solar cells and making use of advances in nanotechnology.

"Breakthroughs Have to Be Made Now"

That wealth of potentially new technologies makes this "an excellent time to put a lot of emphasis on solar energy research," says Walter Kohn, a . . . chemist at the University of California, Santa Barbara. Some of these ideas do currently receive modest funding, enough to support a handful of individual investigator-driven labs. But Richard Smalley, a chemist at Rice University in Houston, Texas, who advocates renewed support for alternative-energy research, notes that unless research progresses far more rapidly to solve the current energy conundrum by 2020, there is essentially no way to have large amounts of clean-energy technology in place by 2050. "That means the basic enabling breakthroughs have to be made now," Smalley says.

Of course a major sticking point is money. At the April meeting, DOE officials started talking about funding a new solar energy research initiative at about $50 million a year, according to Mary Gress, who manages DOE's photochemistry and radiation research. Lewis is reluctant to say how much money is needed but asks rhetorically whether $50 million a year is enough to transform the biggest industry in the world. Clearly, others don't think so. "I don't see any answer that will change it short of an *Apollo*-level program," Smalley says. . . .

At least compared with DOE's earlier push for progress in hydrogen technology, many researchers expect that a push on solar energy research will be a far easier sell. "With hydrogen it was a lot more controversial," Stupp says. "There are scientific issues that are really serious [in getting hydrogen technology to work]. With solar, it's an idea that makes sense in a practical way and is a great source of discovery." If that research and discovery doesn't happen, Lewis says he's worried about what the alternative will bring: "Is this something at which we can afford to fail?"

Solar Power Is Best Suited for Poor Nations

Nicholas Thompson and Ricardo Bayon

In the following selection Nicholas Thompson and Ricardo Bayon argue that it makes more sense to invest in solar technology in developing nations than in technologically advanced countries such as the United States. As an example, they describe the difficulties that villagers in the West African country of Ghana experience trying to obtain electricity. Few electric lines run to rural areas in Africa. Thus, people in developing nations often find that it is more economical to install solar panels than to run power lines to rural communities. The opposite is true in developed nations, which have already installed an extensive electrical grid that reaches nearly all citizens. The authors argue that if developing nations use clean solar energy instead of dirty fossil fuels, the global environment will benefit. Bayon and Thompson are fellows at the New America Foundation, a Washington, D.C.–based public policy foundation.

I n most ways, Patriensa is just another tiny town amidst lush farming land in the Ashanti region of Ghana [in West Africa]: a remote part of a remote country where per-capita income is less than a dollar a day. The day starts when the rooster crows and ends at about 9 P.M., when everyone has finished eating their pounded yams and plantains.

To Osei Darkwa, however, Patriensa is the ideal place to build a technological metropolis. A calm, jovial man who isn't sure whether there are 20 or 30 people living in his house, Darkwa was born in Patriensa, educated in Norway, and able to make a little bit of money working as a professor at the University of Illinois. Now he's come back and is currently building a giant telephone, Internet, and health center, with a radio station and potential data-processing facility for foreign companies to boot. Already, he has shipped hundreds of old computers from the United States, set up computer literacy

The Ashanti region of Ghana in West Africa could benefit from new technologies that provide electricity.

A man uses a cell phone in Botswana, Africa—a rare sight in rural parts of the continent.

courses, found donated hospital beds, and even promised space to an indigenous healer and her potions. He's currently maxing out his American credit cards and cajoling friends and fellow villagers to give free labor and donate land. "It's just a sacrifice for a better tomorrow," he says.

But one thing is stumping him right now: power. The telecenter lies too far away from Ghana's national power grid to receive any electricity, so Darkwa, who needs lights to build his metropolis, has set up solar cells on his roof. Funded partially by an American non-governmental organization, Greenstar, the cells provide enough power for basic lighting and about five computers. Darkwa would like to do more, but he doesn't have the money to buy further cells; getting electricity from the grid means wading and bribing his way through a corrupt and convoluted bureaucracy.

Solar Power Can Reduce Pollution

At first blush, it may not be clear that Darkwa's problem should concern anyone outside Patriensa. But although most Americans couldn't even find Ghana on a map, the energy choices of this small African country, together with those of millions of other people in the developing world, will ultimately affect the environmental, economic, and energy prospects of all Americans. If Darkwa and those like him—some 2 billion energy-starved people around the world—decide to power their televisions and refrigerators with coal and oil, the eventual environmental meltdown will affect every place on earth.

But if wealthier nations can help a large part of their poorer brethren turn to clean and renewable energy, the air will be a lot cleaner, there will be less pollution and poverty, and now trading markets will develop—and the price of oil may even drop. In other words, the United States shouldn't help Darkwa go green merely for his sake, or just because it's a nice thing to do. We should help Darkwa go green because it is profoundly in our own interest.

It may sound far-fetched to ask poor rural communities to adopt solar and renewable energy before rich developed countries. But in fact, solar energy makes vastly more sense in Patriensa than it does in Philadelphia. Americans tend to take electricity for granted. You can buy a hair dryer, plug it in, and turn it on just about anywhere, thanks to a "grid" of generating stations, power lines, and transformers that enmeshes the entire country.

Power Grids Are Insufficient in Developing Nations

But that grid is the product of hundreds of billions of dollars of government subsidies and private investment over the years. In developing countries, by contrast, fully functioning grids tend to be limited to urban areas, are usually nearing obsolescence, or cannot keep up with demand. Most places lack any grid at all. And even if poor countries had the money or inclination to build grids—most have more pressing worries—bringing electricity to small rural villages like Patriensa wouldn't be at the top of their list. As ESKOM, South Africa's largest utility, has discovered, extending the grid to serve a few households often costs significantly more than providing the same village with solar power, and so it has begun to install solar energy in hard-to-reach communities on a monthly-fee basis.

Even where government-built grids are available, there's often a further problem: the government itself. In many developing nations, state-owned or -run utilities are corrupt and unreliable. In Ghana, for example, the one-third of the population that does have access suffers through periodic blackouts, energy spikes, and capricious policies such as a recent 60 percent increase in electricity taxes. The country largely relies upon a single giant dam. When rainfall is low, electricity is low. When a 1998 drought inflicted rolling blackouts, students at the country's top university clustered underneath solar-powered street lamps just off campus to study for their exams.

Solar power and other decentralized sources of energy can help get around these problems. Mobile phones in Africa, Asia, and Latin America provide a hopeful parallel. For decades, people in developing nations had to put up with expensive and poorly designed telephone networks controlled by corrupt and inefficient bureaucrats. But over the past five years, entrepreneurs have built cellular-phone networks that, in effect, circumvent the national telephone system. Five years ago, Ghana didn't have mobile phones. But as a UN [United Nations] task force recently discovered, more cell phone connections have been turned on in Africa in the last five years than land-line connections in the past century.

Economics of Solar Siting

Another reason why solar makes more sense in rural Ghana than downtown D.C. is, simply, competition. In the United States, renewable energy has to compete with highly efficient, cheap, subsidized, and easy-to-find fossil fuels. Burning coal may melt icebergs, but in America it's inexpensive and widely available. Additionally, in the United States we have already invested in the infrastructure needed to transmit electricity from central generating stations to wherever it is needed. So while it costs approximately 2 cents a kilowatt hour to generate electricity from coal, solar energy still costs about 10 times that amount. Of course, solar energy is getting cheaper every day, and burning coal carries longterm health and environmental costs. But in the short term, it makes the most economic sense.

In much of the developing world, on the other hand, burning fossil fuels for electricity doesn't make economic sense—even in the short term—because it would mean investing heavily in infrastructure, transmission capabilities, and generating facilities. (Not to mention the annual costs of buying the necessary fuel.) In other words, for much of the developing world, clean energy competes only with energy generated by burning extremely inefficient, expensive, and difficult-to-find fuels. For these people, solar power would cost less over the long term than what they spend now collecting or buying firewood, kerosene, candles, and dry-cell batteries. In Morocco, for instance, "more than half of the people who live off-grid already spend close to $100 dollars a year" on such fuels, notes Vikram Widge, a renewable-energy

A giant mirror traps the sun's rays to generate steam for cooking community meals in Auroville, India.

expert at the International Finance Corporation, the private-sector arm of the World Bank. "Meanwhile, a solar home system of 50 watts—enough to run two or three light bulbs, an electrical outlet, a TV, and maybe a fan—costs about $550 but has an estimated lifetime of 20 years." . . .

[I]f developing countries rely mostly on traditional energy sources as they grow, they will begin to compete with the United States for oil and gas. China, for instance, currently uses coal for about 70 percent of its energy needs. But by 2030, estimates the

International Energy Agency, China's demand for oil will equal that of the United States, making it a strategic buyer on world energy markets. The emergence of China as a new "energy giant", says the IEA, will have an impact on the energy security of all other energy consuming countries. And, depending on how India's economy grows, it too could one day compete with the United States for imported oil. Simple economic theory indicates that as the demand for a commodity increases (assuming that supply remains stable), so too will its price. In other words, by helping developing countries adopt solar and wind energy, the United States may be helping hold down its own oil bill.

The Environmental Benefits of Solar Power

The main benefits to the United States from clean energy in the developing world are, however, environmental. While global energy use is expected to grow at an average rate of about 1.7 percent per year in the decades to come, it will likely increase more than twice as fast in developing ones, and even faster than that in China. Over the coming decades, China and India will need to provide energy to millions of peasants who, like those in Timber Nkwanta, are miles away from the nearest electrical line. If China and India meet that demand by expanding their grids and burning more coal—both have plentiful coal supplies—and biomass, the resulting pollution will make the brown cloud that has been stifling parts of Asia this year look like cigarette smoke on a windy day. But with some help from the international community, it would be cheaper to provide solar electricity to these multitudes than to extend grids to reach them—and better for the environment, too.

CHAPTER 3

The Future of Solar Energy

Visitors wait to tour a modular solar house entered in the 2005 Solar Decathlon in Washington, D.C.

American Homes Will Use More Solar Energy

Joe Provey

> In the following selection Joe Provey explains that solar energy is becoming a routine part of home building in the United States. Even though it remains relatively expensive to generate electricity with photovoltaic cells, the technology is gaining popularity. After many years in which most of the photovoltaic cells produced in the United States were shipped to other countries, residential use of solar generation in America is growing by over 25 percent or more a year, Provey writes. Although the cost of electricity produced by such systems is today substantially higher than that provided by local utilities, many homeowners think that home solar systems can be a good hedge against future rises in energy prices. Provey is a writer whose books and articles address a wide variety of lifestyle topics.

The dream of solar energy and what it implies—cheap power, clean air, independence from foreign oil producers—has been around for a long time. But now, the dream may finally be coming true. Solar electricity, also called photovoltaic (PV) energy, is fast becoming a viable option for homeowners who want to generate their own power. A technology developed to power satellites in the 1950s, PV energy had been too expensive for most residential applications until recently. Concerns with rising energy costs, power disruptions, pollution and global

Joe Provey, "The Sun Also Rises—Again," *Popular Mechanics*, September 10, 2002. Reproduced by permission.

warming have combined with reductions in the cost of PV cells, improved technology, government incentives and solar-friendly legislation to make solar power shine brighter than it has for decades.

Although the U.S. solar power industry went through hard times in the last 25 years, it didn't die. Instead, it retreated to overseas markets. In recent years, more than 75 percent of American-produced solar cells—the key component of a PV system—have been exported. Some went to developing countries where photovoltaic systems are used for lighting, powering telecommunications systems, and pumping water for crop irrigation and domestic needs in remote villages. Others went to industrial countries, especially Japan and Germany, where there are strong incentives to put solar electricity (and solar hot water) in homes, schools, and commercial and municipal buildings. As the technology improved, the solar industry began to find niche markets in the United States, including traffic control and message boards, TV, radio and cellular repeater stations, and navigational buoys and beacons. Add it all up and you have an industry approaching $4 billion in global sales.

The Solar Industry Is Growing

By all accounts, PV energy won't stop there. Allen Barnett, chief executive officer of AstroPower, a fast-growing producer of solar cells and solar electric power systems for residential applications, says that the PV industry is growing by 25 to 30 percent a year. AstroPower's capacity is growing faster to keep up with demand. Plant expansions have brought the company's production capability from 35 megawatts in 2000 (a megawatt equals 1000 kilowatts, enough energy to power hundreds of homes) to 110 megawatts projected by the end of 2002—a total that would have been unthinkable just a few years ago.

John Schaeffer, founder of Real Goods Trading Co. (now called Gaiam Real Goods after a recent merger), has been selling solar products for more than 20 years. He confirms that the hot growth area today is on-site generation of electricity—either by solar or wind power. "Events such as . . . California's

Buildings in Soldier's Grove, Wisconsin, use solar power, a resource that is gaining popularity across the United States.

rolling blackouts in 2000, recent spikes in energy costs and ongoing unrest in the Middle East have spurred interest in self-sufficiency and have also spurred growth."

National homebuilding companies have become interested in adding PV to their homes' selling features. Shea Homes, the

Solar Power House

A basic photovoltaic system starts with solar-collecting panels on the roof that generate the direct current (DC) electricity. This current then moves to an inverter that changes it to the alternating current (AC) required for the house. From this inverter, the current moves into the electrical-service panel for distribution.

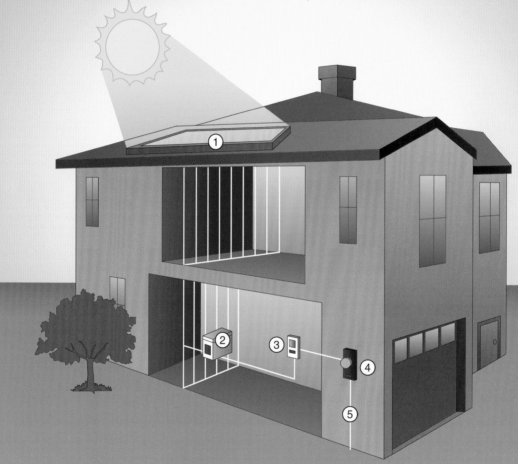

1. Solar panels convert sunlight into DC electric power.
2. Inverter converts DC power into standard household AC power for use in the home.
3. Existing electrical panel distributes solar electricity and utility power to loads in the house.
4. Utility meter spins backward when solar-electricity generation exceeds house-electricity consumption. Power is sold back to the utility at the utility's retail price.
5. Utility power is automatically provided at night and during the day when demand exceeds solar production.

10th-largest builder in the United States, and Pardee Homes are installing PV systems in hundreds of new homes under construction in various San Diego communities. U.S. Home, a division of Lennar Corp., plans to build more than 900 PV-energized homes in 2003 at its Bickford Ranch development near Sacramento.

There are cost efficiencies to integrating PV installations with the normal workflow of home construction, according to Jonathan Done, a spokesman for Shea. "We are able to offer buyers systems for $6000 to $10,000, depending upon the size, after Shea takes care of getting the state rebates," he says, "and the homeowner can take an additional 15 percent state income tax credit." By comparison, installations on existing homes typically cost 50 percent more. Home sales with PV have been brisk, Done says. "The feature certainly does not hinder sales, and may be helping."

Available off the Rack

In 2001, The Home Depot decided to offer packaged PV systems, pre-engineered by AstroPower, at select outlets in the San Diego area. The systems are sold under The Home Depot's Installed Products program. If sales go well, PV products may be rolled out to as many as 70 Home Depot stores in California and eventually to other strong solar power markets across the country.

Earning Money from Solar Panels

Another reason for the PV industry growth is "net metering," a protocol that allows homeowners to be credited for the electricity they produce. It works like this: When a homeowner produces more electricity than he or she is using—typically during the middle of most weekdays when usage is low—it's fed back into the power grid. In this reverse mode, the homeowner's analog electric meter literally spins backward.

When usage outstrips production or when the sun sets and rooftop electricity can no longer be produced, PV homeowners draw from the utility company. But PV homeowners on the net-metering system pay only for the net amount of electricity they use. In effect, they are being credited for their production at the same retail price they would normally pay the utility company. In states with tiered electric rates—where homeowners pay a higher rate per kilowatt once their usage surpasses set thresholds—the credit pays for the most costly kilowatt-hours.

In the dozen or so states where net-metering legislation has not been enacted, homeowners may still connect to the grid but they won't get credit for their excess daytime production. Instead they will have to store it in a bank of batteries. Batteries have been successfully used for decades, but they add expense, lower system efficiency, require maintenance and monitoring, and introduce hazardous chemicals into the home environment. To learn more about net metering in your state, visit www.dsireusa.org.

Falling Costs

Another reason for the increasing interest in solar electricity is steep reductions in the cost of PV cells—the basic units from which PV solar modules are made. According to Barnett of AstroPower, the cost for PV cells is halved roughly every 10 years. Though manufactured from one of the most common elements on Earth, silicon, solar cells are not cheap. The retail cost is between $4.50 and $7 per watt of rated capacity, or about $600 for one 100-watt module. The cost is high because the conventional way of manufacturing cells is fairly complex. First, large silicon crystals have to be grown, typically in cylindrical forms. These ingots, or loaves, are then sliced with lasers into wafers of pure crystal before becoming the basis for a solar cell.

Several companies have developed ways to lower cost and speed production of solar cells. They have, for example, found that it's easier and less expensive to grow multicrystalline, or polycrystalline, materials (masses of smaller crystals). These cells are nearly as efficient as those made with single crystals.

Other companies have experimented with thin-film technologies in which silicon material is vaporized and deposited in very thin layers on various substrates, including glass and flexible backings. These amorphous solar cells have opened the possibility for creating innovative products, such as electricity-

An employee and customer discuss products at Home Depot. The store chain launched a program to get customers to buy solar power systems.

generating windows, roofing and siding. While thin-film products are typically less efficient than single- or multicrystalline cells, they cost significantly less. . . .

The Customer

The typical PV consumer is someone who is comfortable with new technology and who lives in a state with lots of sun, high electric rates and favorable government incentives. Rick Elmore, a manager for a telecommunications company who lives in

Poway, Calif., could be a poster child for the PV industry. Last summer, he signed up for The Home Depot's pilot program to add a 2400-watt AstroPower SunLine PV system to his 1750-sq.-ft. frame and stucco house, which was built in 1975. Elmore says he was an ideal candidate because he pays 13 cents per kilowatt-hour, his home gets lots of sun, and he has just enough area for 24 100-watt modules on his south-facing roof. The installation, which, after rebate and tax deduction, cost about $15,000, supplies nearly all of his electrical needs. His most recent electric bill was only $5.46. What's more, Elmore has fixed his electricity costs. If the price of a kilowatt-hour rises in the coming years, it will barely affect what he pays for electricity. . . .

How long it takes to see a return on your money depends largely on the incentives offered in your state and other variables such as system cost, usage, electric rates, climate and the interest rate you obtain to finance the setup.

Improved Solar Water Heaters Could Lead to Solar Air Conditioning

John Colmey

In the selection that follows, John Colmey describes the simplified design that Malaysian inventor and architect Teoh Siang Teik has created for solar water heaters. Teoh's effort to make a simpler, better, and cheaper solar water heater began in 1979. Over the next two decades, Teoh continued to make improvements on his water heater design, leading to a solar water heater that is, according to Colmey, far superior to anything that had been previously produced. Teoh's water heater can be built from off-the-shelf hardware, needs no electricity to operate, and brings water to a temperature of as much as 78°C (172°F), well above the 60°C (140°F) maximum of previous models. Getting water to that temperature using only solar energy makes it technically feasible to design a solar-powered air conditioner for homes. Such a development could greatly improve the lives of people living in tropical areas of developing countries, where electricity is scarce and costly. Colmey is a Malaysia-based correspondent for *Time International*.

Teoh Siang Teik didn't set out to design the world's most powerful solar water heater. He just wanted to go trekking. As an architecture student in Scotland in 1979, the young Malaysian was looking for a way to prolong a visit to Nepal when a local businessman asked him to design a hotel in a rural area with no electricity. His energy-efficient solution won first prize from Scotland's Royal Incorporation of Architects. He returned with his architecture degree and designed 69 rural buildings for the Nepalese government, incorporating solar water heating. "My professors had told me to leave engineering to engineers and be an architect," Teoh recalls. "I was just looking for a way to save money on materials."

Finding a More Efficient Way to Heat Water

That quest resulted in a stunningly simple engineering breakthrough. At the time, there was essentially one way to build solar

The buildings Teoh Siang Teik designed for rural areas of Nepal (pictured) incorporate solar water heating.

water heaters, using a 1976 Japanese patent that is still commonly applied today. In that basic design, an array of tubes in a flat glass panel is placed on a slope or roof and connected to a water tank. The water in the tubes is heated by the sun, rises slowly and enters a pipe running across the top of the panel, where it pushes forward and empties into the tank. The circle is completed when cold water is forced out of the bottom of the tank into a pipe running to the bottom of the panel. From there it begins the journey through the panel and back up to the tank again. Standing on the roof of one his houses in Nepal, Teoh was watching the hot water rise and shoot into a black 55-gallon drum when he realized how much heat was being lost pushing the water through the system. Says Teoh: "The first rule of solar water heating was that the tank was separate from the panel" and connected by a single tube. "I knew there had to be a more efficient way."

There was. After pondering the problem for several years, Teoh designed a heater in which each tube in the panel pours hot water directly into the tank. That shortens the path the water has to travel by nearly a meter and thus slashes the energy loss in transport. Building on the notion of reducing resistance to hot water flow, Teoh's research over the next decade led to several more design improvements. For example, he added an additional lower panel with exposed tubes suspended over a mirror that allows the heater to receive additional sunlight and even work on a cloudy day.

Teoh's Solar Water Heater Beats the Competition

Teoh's solar water heater, which was granted one of three international patents issued by the World Intellectual Property Organization (under the Patent Cooperation Treaty) in 1997, out-performs the competition. It guarantees a water temperature of 60–78 [degrees] C—as opposed to the previous 50–60 [degrees] C ceiling—more than enough for an entire family of five to take two hot showers a day. Unlike other solar water heaters, it doesn't need an electric-powered backup, which on cloudy days can make operating costs skyrocket. And Teoh's model can be built using materials available at a local hardware store. Such simplicity allows the company Teoh has set up in his home, Microsolar Malaysia, to sell heaters for as little as $1,000. That's one-third the cost of a more technologically sophisticated solar model designed by the U.S. National Aeronautics and Space Administration. Teoh's design not only produces hot water without burning fossil fuels, but it operates more cheaply than other solar models. In the first 10 years, his heater costs a family of five $100 annually, compared with $200 for a conventional solar unit with an electric booster and just under that for an all-electric model. "It works," says one of Microsolar Malaysia's 1,000 customers, Affendy Th'ng, a Kuala Lumpur sales executive. Affendy went solar to help the environment and to avoid buying individual electric heaters for his three bathrooms. He now enjoys "a substantial savings on my monthly bill."

On to Air Conditioners

More importantly, Teoh's innovation could unlock many more, including solar air-conditioners. Until now, finding an efficient way to use the sun's energy to cool air has eluded engineers because the water temperature must be maintained at an average 75[degrees]C in order to run existing solar air-conditioning models. Currently, five to eight panels are required to reach that temperature, far too cumbersome and costly for a typical roof, where Microsolar could potentially do it with two to four panels. Many air-conditioners now use a volatile gas like freon, which is known to contribute to global warming. So a freon-free model could be a boon for the environment, as well as an important new industry for Malaysia, already a major manufacturer of air-conditioners.

Though Teoh has gained international recognition for his stroke of solar engineering, he remains very much an architect, designing buildings throughout Asia. Microsolar Malaysia plans

Air conditioners, which use freon gas, could one day be powered by solar energy to create their cooling effects.

to franchise his low-cost water heaters to the developing world, beginning with Botswana this year [1998]. Nonetheless, Teoh rejects the notion that he is a hero. "I don't the like the word," says the inventor. "I just want to be somebody who makes a small contribution to the world." And if he is lucky, he may still have time to go trekking, although the demands of fame are making that increasingly difficult.

Solar and Hydrogen Energy Will Power Future Homes

David G. Schieren

Every year the U.S. Department of Energy sponsors a competition to design the most attractive and efficient solar-powered home. In the selection that follows, David G. Schieren, leader of one of the competing teams, testifies before a congressional committee about the challenges and advantages of his team's design. Schieren, representing a team from the New York Institute of Technology and the U.S. Merchant Marine Academy, explains that their home uses photovoltaic panels to convert sunlight into electricity, which powers the home when the sun is shining. Some of the electricity is used to extract hydrogen from water, and the hydrogen gas is then stored for use in a fuel cell. When the sun is not shining, the hydrogen powers a fuel cell, which produces electricity for the home. Schieren is a graduate student in energy management at the New York Institute of Technology.

It is a great honor to present the New York Institute of Technology's (NYIT) and the US Merchant Marine Academy's (USMMA) Solar-Hydrogen Home, our 2005 Solar Decathlon Entry, to the [congressional] Subcommittee on Energy. My name is David Schieren and I am graduate energy management student from NYIT. With me today is Heather

David G. Schieren, "2005 Solar Decathlon: Congressional Testimony," *U.S. House of Representatives Committee on Science*, Subcommittee on Energy, November 2, 2005. Reproduced by permission of the author.

Korb, lead architect from NYIT and Greg Sachs, lead engineer from the USMMA. For the past 2 years NYIT and the USMMA have been working on an extraordinary project—an advanced Solar Hydrogen home. We strongly believe that solar energy, renewable hydrogen and sustainable design offer a future of true energy independence, a clean environment, and greatly enhanced civilization. . . .

NYIT's Solar Home is called Green Machine/Blue Space. Green Machine [GM], the life support of the house and Blue Space, the dwelling place, are two parts working together as one self-sustaining unit.

Visitors take cover in the rain during the 2005 Solar Decathlon, a competition to design, build, and operate the most livable solar-powered house.

GM is a modified shipping container that houses the mechanics of life including a kitchen, a bathroom, roof garden for food production, solar water heating, and hydrogen production and storage. Containers are ubiquitous, and we consider them a premade space—structurally sound and easily transported by rail, air and sea. This system is ideal for numerous applications, including disaster relief, and military uses.

Blue Space is a site-specific design that emphasizes dwelling quality and sustainability through materials selection, efficiency, passive solar strategies and natural ventilation. Through design, the energy load was minimized, reducing the on-site power requirements.

Power Systems: Solar-Hydrogen

Solar panels are the primary source of energy, and a hydrogen fuel cell is used for nighttime energy requirements. Solar panels con-

A tube-shaped, solar-powered house attracts attention at the 2005 Solar Decathlon in Washington, D.C.

vert sunlight into electricity and send it to the house loads. Surplus solar energy is sent to a hydrogen generator that produces hydrogen gas from water. When there is no sunlight, the fuel cell converts the hydrogen gas back into electricity to power the house. This is a quiet and clean process: The fuel-cell byproducts are water and heat, and the water is used again and converted back into hydrogen, creating a regenerative cycle. . . .

This is a vital demonstration project: Applying these technologies will help determine how to improve it. Hydrogen produced in this way can replace fossil fuels and end dependency on foreign nations for our energy supplies. Hydrogen gas is superior to and more versatile than other energy storage technologies, such as batteries. This is the model of a new energy paradigm, a distributed generation energy system—inherently stronger than the centralized and interdependent system of today.

My testimony today will specifically address the subcommittee's questions:

Q: Given your experience, what do you think are the main technical and other barriers to greater use of solar energy?

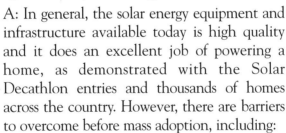

A: In general, the solar energy equipment and infrastructure available today is high quality and it does an excellent job of powering a home, as demonstrated with the Solar Decathlon entries and thousands of homes across the country. However, there are barriers to overcome before mass adoption, including:

- Lack of education and public awareness about the benefits of solar energy and the true costs of the current fossil fuel based system to the environment and national security.
- The high cost and short supply of solar panels and raw materials.
- The inconsistency, and uncertainty of government incentives.
- Lack of training for engineers, construction workers, architects, business people, bankers.

- Lack of incentives for new property developers to incorporate into structures.
- Utility opposition in certain regions. . . .

Q: Do you have any suggestions for what might be done to overcome those barriers?

A: The government is supporting the development of solar and hydrogen technologies to some extent. We would advise increasing this investment and setting out a clear vision—a bold national strategy—with specific milestones that lead towards a clean and renewable energy economy.

Q: How do you see the competition itself as helping to move both solar and efficiency technologies into the mainstream building market?

A: This high-profile competition had a deeply positive impact on helping to move solar and efficiency technologies into the mainstream building market. The core challenge of the Solar Decathlon is to build a beautiful and energy self-sufficient home. At our school, this challenge inspired over 100 students and faculty from the architecture, engineering, interior design, and communications departments to work together to integrate a design vision with engineering and construction realities. The knowledge and experience gained from this project will carry with us as we become the next generation of leaders in our respective fields, and the impact extends from all the decathletes to our families, friends, and colleagues. Through fundraising and PR [public relations] efforts, our ideas were shared with many leading figures in the building and energy fields, in addition to countless homeowners. While still at school, people from the community would stop by the site and ask how they too could use solar technologies. While on the National Mall during the event, the flow of people—and the interest they had in solar and efficiency technologies—was breathtaking. Everyone wanted "solar" today. . . .

Q: Would your house be commercially viable? If not, what changes would make it more attractive to the mainstream home buyers?

A: With solar power and energy efficient design technologies, it often comes down to a cost/benefit analysis: Is the upfront investment worth the long-term benefits? Is it worth the wait? The

People interested in saving energy explore a model of a solar-powered home.

NYIT house with the hydrogen fuel cell system is not commercially viable today—though this is what we are working towards. The solar electric and solar hot water systems are because of the incentives that our local utility, the Long Island Power Authority, offer. However, this still requires a large upfront investment. With regard to the house itself and its design, it is the market that determines whether the product is "commercially viable." Based on interactions with numerous people, we do think that our house is attractive to mainstream home buyers.

Satellites Will Supply the Earth with Solar Energy

Ralph H. Nansen

In the selection that follows, Ralph H. Nansen takes readers on an imaginary tour of a solar-power satellite. The satellite he envisions would be a vast, orbiting structure in space. It would gather up solar energy, convert it to electricity, and then turn the electricity into radio waves that would carry the energy down to Earth for use in homes, businesses, and factories. The entire structure, orbiting high above the United States, would need only minor upkeep, Nansen says, and would be virtually undetectable from Earth. Nansen, a former Boeing space engineer, is president of Solar Space Industries. In 2000 he testified before a congressional committee about his vision of a government-industry project to launch the first solar-power satellite.

L et me take you on a tour of a solar power satellite. . . . As we approach the satellite we see a huge rectangular array of solar cells stretching into the distance, bathed in dazzling sunlight. A shining jewel in the blackness of space. Its frame is hidden in the shadow of the solar array, and at one end is a giant flat disk, textured with millions of small rectangular slots to focus the energy streaming toward the earth 22,300 miles below.

Our first impression of the satellite would be its gigantic size. A few years ago while on a business trip to New York, I was suddenly struck with the magnitude of size. On a brilliantly clear day I sat in a reception room on the fiftieth floor of one of New York's modern office buildings. I looked out over Manhattan Island and realized that a single satellite would cover half of the sea of buildings before me. It was a sobering vision that dramatically impressed me with how large a solar power satellite would actually be—a rectangle of nearly twenty square miles (fifty square kilometers), paved entirely with solar cells. . . .

The Satellite Will Be Unnoticeable from Earth

Even though the satellite is vast, it will not cast a shadow on the earth. Most of the year, the tilt of the earth's axis causes the

Pictured is a satellite image of New York City. Some envision a satellite that can convert solar energy to electricity and beam it to Earth.

satellite to pass either above or below the earth's shadow. During this same time, as the satellite's orbit takes it toward the sun from the earth, its shadow would also pass above or below the earth. During the equinox period, when the earth's axis is perpendicular to the sun, the satellite will pass between the earth and the sun. However, even then its shadow won't pass over the earth because of an interesting phenomenon of light. As an object is moved away from the earth toward the very large sphere of the sun, the sunlight passing on one side of the object will converge with the light passing on the other and there will be no shadow.

Also, despite the satellite's size, it won't be visible from earth during the day. The question of visibility depends upon several factors including distance, size, and reflectivity. I have already discussed its size and altitude, so the remaining question is how much light will it reflect. During the daylight hours, the satellite is oriented toward the sun, away from the observer, while the dark side is facing the earth, just like the new moon. We cannot see the new moon during the day and will not be able to see the satellite either.

After dark, the story will be different. With the satellite on the opposite side of the earth from the sun, it will reflect light back toward the earth like the moon. However, since the surface is covered with solar cells that absorb light while converting sunlight to electricity, there will probably be just enough reflected light to make the satellite as visible as an average star. On a clear night, we should be able to see a starry string of pearls—with each satellite representing one pearl—glowing in the night sky.

The Satellite Will Not Fall to Earth

When I speak to the public about solar power satellites, one of the questions I can always expect is this: "*Skylab* fell back to the earth; since the solar power satellite is so big, won't it fall too?"

Skylab was America's first large space station and was placed in a low-earth orbit. Low-earth orbit extends from about 75 miles altitude up to 400 miles. Manned systems in low-earth orbit are placed within a maximum of 400 miles because of the radiation in the Van Allen Belt above that altitude. The initial orbit of *Skylab* when it was launched in 1973 was about 270

Some worry that a large satellite that provides solar power could eventually fall back to Earth as the Skylab *space station (pictured) did in 1979.*

miles above the earth, over 22,000 miles closer to earth's gravity and atmosphere than the solar power satellite will be.

We think of the atmosphere as having a finite end, but it does not. It simply becomes less and less dense until finally it is gone. There was a very thin layer of atmosphere in the *Skylab* orbit, which produced some drag and gradually reduced its speed with atmospheric friction. With the speed decrease, altitude was lost. As *Skylab* drifted into lower altitudes the atmosphere became denser and eventually friction caused the satellite to burn as it reentered the dense atmosphere. If there had been enough fuel on board to make course corrections, it would still be in orbit.

In the case of a solar power satellite in geosynchronous orbit, the atmosphere is nonexistent so the satellite will not be subjected to atmospheric drag. Satellites at that altitude will stay there for hundreds of thousands of years. There is no danger of a satellite falling from geosynchronous orbit.

The Satellite's Structure

As we move behind the satellite and look underneath the vast expanse of solar cells we see a spidery framework of triangular-truss beams that form the satellite's skeleton. It's a rectangular framework, divided into 500-meter-square bays, providing the foundation for mounting all of the other elements and defining the satellite's shape and size. Triangular trusses have proven to be the lightest, most efficient skeleton for very large structures. The great rigid dirigibles built in the early part of the century used aluminum triangular trusses for their structure, and most radio and television antenna towers are truss beams. Such beams are ideally suited for the structure of the satellite, which must be very large and rigid, but will be lightly loaded.

An alternative structural approach we have been looking at for the new smaller models (1,000 megawatts) would use a tetrahedron space frame made of tapered aluminum tubes. A tetrahedron looks like a pyramid with a strut at each corner and around the bottom. All of the struts are the same length, and when you join these pyramids together by adding struts to the tops it becomes a space frame. . . .

There are several choices of materials that could be used for the structure, but the most likely will be aluminum. It is lightweight, easy to work, inexpensive, and has the great advantage of long life. The satellite structure would be designed to last indefinitely. Only the power generator and transmitter would require regular maintenance, probably on an annual basis by robotic means supported by maintenance personnel living on a nearby space station.

Advanced composite materials might reduce the weight and increase the rigidity of the satellite, but there are still some unanswered questions about their longevity in the space environment. NASA [National Aeronautics and Space Administration] has been testing a number of new composite materials in space for several years, but until sufficient time has passed to determine life capabilities, aluminum remains the best choice.

Solar Cells Do the Work

If the structure of the satellite is its skeleton, then solar cells are the muscles that do the work. When we look at the cells closely we see smooth, flat, blue-black wafers with a fine grid pattern on their surface to collect the electricity that is generated when sunlight releases electrons within the cell. They convert 16.5% of the sunlight to electricity and are only two thousandths of an inch thick, which is no thicker than a sheet of paper.

In 1978, my Boeing study team faced quite a challenge trying to decide which solar cells to use in our research. At that time there were several different types being developed, but the most common were single crystal silicon cells and gallium arsenide cells. After many sessions with some talented aerospace engineers, the decision was made to use single crystal silicon cells because of their proven performance, light weight, and demonstrated efficiency. The engineers at Rockwell International, who were also studying solar cell choices at the same time, chose gallium arsenide for their studies. Their decision was to explore the potential of more advanced, higher efficiency cells. Our selection was more conservative—we knew the cells were readily available and would work.

As we look at the satellite you can see that the solar cells are assembled into conveniently sized panels, one meter square. What you can't see is how the cells in each panel are interconnected using 14 cells in parallel with each parallel group connected in series to the next group. This provides very high reliability since any four cells in parallel can be lost before the panel stops operating. If a meteorite struck the satellite, it would only experience power loss in the damaged cell area. Based on NASA's meteorite density data, the study team projected a loss of less than 1% of the cells over a 30-year period. The new models will have even higher reliability as they will use the technique developed by the terrestrial solar cell industry of bypass diodes to provide for an alternate electrical path. Each panel would be interconnected like the squares of a quilt to fill each structural bay. These in turn are joined together to create the rectangular form of the satellite.

Great strides have been made in solar cell development since the 1970s, and there are now many good cell materials from which to choose. Single crystal silicon is still the most common, multi-layer gallium arsenide are still the highest efficiency, but thin-film cells made from cadmium telluride, copper-indium-deselenide, or multi-layer amorphous silicon are lighter weight and less expensive, but also less efficient. The decision for the future must be made whether to build a large satellite with many low-cost cells or a smaller satellite using fewer, but more expensive cells. Another way to reduce the number of cells required is by using concentrators, such as mirrors or lenses, to focus the sunlight from a large area to a smaller area of solar cells. Regardless of the type of solar cell material selected, the cells would be installed in a way similar to the efficient arrangement worked out in the 1970s studies—a smooth and shiny quilt in the darkness of space. . . .

How the Satellite Is Aligned with the Sun

Because the solar cells must always point toward the sun while the transmitting antenna points toward the earth, the connecting joint will make one revolution each day. At the same time, this joint must also provide for the transmission of eight billion watts of electrical output from the solar cells to the transmitter. Unfortunately, wires cannot be used as they would soon twist off due to the continuous rotating motion. Slip-rings, similar to those used in some electric motors and radar sets, but on a much larger scale, would work well here. Since the motion is slow, there should be very little wear. As a comparison, the engine of an automobile will make more revolutions during a 15-minute drive to the grocery store than the antenna will make in a hundred years.

The task of keeping the satellite pointing toward the sun will be performed by an attitude control system. The attitude control systems for the Space Shuttle and for some of the current satellite systems burn small amounts of chemical propellants in tiny rockets to turn and position the spacecraft to the desired

Solar Power Satellites

Solar power satellites could supply Earth with electricity in the following ways:

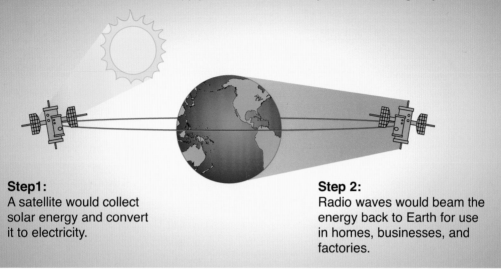

Step1:
A satellite would collect solar energy and convert it to electricity.

Step 2:
Radio waves would beam the energy back to Earth for use in homes, businesses, and factories.

position. However, on the solar power satellites we can take advantage of electricity to power ion thrusters to accelerate an inert gas (most likely argon) to very high velocity, thus creating a rocket-thrust reaction. . . .

The Transmitting Antenna

As we turn our attention to the transmitting antenna we see that it is mounted on a rotary joint at one end of the satellite and faces the earth at all times. It seems small compared to the rest of the satellite, although a disk one kilometer (0.62 miles) in diameter is large by most standards. Closer inspection reveals the disk to be covered with aluminum planks. As we take a still closer look we see that the planks are covered with slots, which are actually slotted wave guides. Wave guides are hollow rectangular box sections that channel radio-frequency energy so it can radiate out through the slots in the front face of the guides. This design concept is identical to many large phased-array radars in use today. The difference would be in the specific frequency used and in the fact that radar sets transmit energy in pulses, receiving reflected signals between pulses. By contrast, energy from the satellite would be continuously transmitted. The term "phased array" means that the beam formation and steering comes from control of the radio-frequency waves across the face of the transmitter.

As we make our way to the backside of the antenna we see it is cluttered with supporting structure and with electronic equipment generating radio-frequency energy. The transmitter is the most complex part of the satellite system with two important functions to perform. It must convert electric energy generated by the solar cells to radio-frequency energy and it must form the beam. . . .

Transmission of the energy to earth is the last function the satellite needs to accomplish to fulfill its role as a solar power plant. Control of the beam is accomplished by controlling the frequency phasing of the radio waves over the face of the antenna. This in turn requires controlling the phasing of each individual microwave generator in relation to its neighbor.

Satellite Vulnerability

From our brief tour, you can see the elegant simplicity of the design, but before leaving the subject of the satellite itself, I want to address one often-raised question about the vulnerability of the solar satellite. . . .

The location of the solar power satellites is a strong deterrent to attack. Access to geosynchronous orbit is difficult to achieve, and even with modern rockets it is a journey of over five hours. High-powered laser weapons could conceivably be used in the future, but they require high technology and a large sustained power output that is difficult to achieve.

Vandals or terrorists would also find it very difficult to attack a solar power satellite. Even the receiving antenna on earth would prove to be a frustrating target because of its great size.

If the United States were the only nation to possess solar power satellites, we could be in a situation envied by other nations and in that case it might be prudent to consider defending them from attack. However, the best defense is to make energy from solar power satellites available to all who need it. The energy crisis is not only an American crisis but a world crisis as well. Global access to energy from space would benefit all nations and preclude a threat of war.

Solar Energy Will Make Drinking Water Safe in Remote Areas

Trudy C. Rolla

> In the following selection environmental health expert
> Trudy C. Rolla explains how various simple solar devices are
> beginning to make drinking water safer in remote locations.
> As an example, she describes Masai villagers in Kenya, who
> often suffer diarrhea because of microbes in their water. An
> Irish team of researchers made a simple device for them that
> kills germs by exposing them to sunlight. Other low-tech
> solar water purifiers work by heating the water. To purify
> large quantities of water for whole villages, some companies
> have made solar stills with valves and filters that distill
> water. Rolla is a health and environmental investigator for
> King County in the state of Washington.

In [some] parts of the world, the sun is a constant, reliable
presence, while water, especially safe drinking water, is
chancy. Unsafe drinking water causes the majority of deaths
and diseases in developing countries. People have long used
the sun for cooking and preserving food. The sun's energy can
also be used to heat water to pasteurization temperature, which
kills most pathogens. Many devices have been developed that
concentrate the sun's energy. These devices can be as simple as
a black box with a pot in it, or as complex as solar-powered
battery cells that provide electricity for ultraviolet (UV) or

oxidation systems. Most of the simple devices are not intended to "sterilize" water, but to reduce the number of pathogens so that the water is safer to drink.

How Solar Boxes Work

The simplest solar water purification devices are the solar box and the solar still. Solar boxes are a well-known method for cooking food and can be used for water pasteurization. A solar box consists of a cardboard or wooden box with insulated bottom and sides and a glass or clear-plastic lid. The inside surfaces should be painted black. A covered pot with water (ideally, also black) is placed inside. The pot needs to remain in the box until the water is at 150 [degrees] F (65 [degrees] C) for a few minutes. Generally, a solar box can pasteurize about 1 gallon of water in 3 hours on a very sunny day in, say, southern California. Pasteurization kills bacteria, viruses, and cysts, but does not remove chemical contaminants.

A very low-tech method, using direct solar radiation to reduce pathogens, was field-tested by researchers from the Royal College of Surgeons in Dublin, Ireland. The researchers gave 206 Masai children clear, 1.5-liter plastic bottles. The children in the test group were told to fill the bottles (from the contaminated water supply) and place them on the roof, from dawn to midday. The control group kept their bottles inside. Diarrhea incidence in the two groups was tracked over 12 weeks. The researchers found that this solar radiation method may significantly reduce diarrheal disease for communities that have no other way to disinfect water.

A Simple Safety Indicator

Boiling water is not necessary to kill pathogens, but reaching water pasteurization temperature is critical. So how do you measure temperature, especially in a remote area, after the glass thermometer breaks? An ingenious solution is the Water Pasteurization Indicator (WAPI). A prototype was developed by Dr. Fred Barrett (U.S. Department of Agriculture, retired) in 1988. The current WAPI was developed by Dale Andreatta and other graduate engineering students at the University of California, Berkeley. The WAPI is a polycarbonate tube, sealed at both ends, and partially filled with a blue soybean fat that melts at 156 [degrees] F (69 [degrees] C). The WAPI is placed inside the water container, with the fat end up. The user can easily tell when the water reaches 156 [degrees] F (69 [degrees] C) because the fat melts and runs to the bottom of the tube. The WAPI is reusable and durable. This device can be placed in a pot in a solar box or over a stove or fire. Since pasteurization occurs at a lower temperature than boiling, less fuel is needed for heating water. This is important where fuel is scarce or expensive.

Women in Mali, Africa, wash pots and collect water from the Niger River. A solar box can provide the energy to sanitize drinking water in rural areas.

If materials for a box are not available, or if cost is a factor, then a solar puddle may be the answer. A shallow pit about 3 feet (1 meter) square and 4 inches deep is dug and is insulated with native materials (paper, straw, grass, leaves). Over this are placed layers of clear and then black plastic, with the edges extending out and over the sides of the pit. The bottom should be flat, except for a trough along one side. A WAPI could go in the trough, the coolest part. A drain siphon is installed in the lowest part of the trough, and weighted down with rocks. Water is added to a depth of 1 to 3 inches. A layer of clear plastic is laid over the water, with the edges extending over the edges of the pit. Spacers, such as wadded paper, are placed on this layer of plastic. Then a final layer of plastic is placed over the spacers; the plastic layers should be at least 2 inches apart. Rocks and dirt are used to weigh down the edges of the plastic. Water needs to be added each day. During tests in Berkeley, sunny days produced 17 gallons of water in the device, which cost about $4.

A higher-tech version of the solar box was developed by Sun Utility Network, Inc. They produce a Sun Thermos Bottle, essentially an oversized insulated tube. They claim that it will kill bacteria, protozoa, and viruses as it reaches pasteurization temperature. A single bottle lists for $150, and Sun Utility also offers accessories such as containers, filters, and stand. The company is offering cash awards and marketing assistance to developers of simple, practical, and cost-effective applications of their product for developing countries, campsites, or eco-tourist developments.

Solar Stills

The concept of a solar still is familiar to anyone who has been inside a steamy greenhouse. A solar still usually consists of a large flat surface, about the size of a dining room table (about 3 by 5 feet). This can be mounted on legs or on top of a shed or house. A short wall is built around the top of the table and is lined with impermeable material (ideally black, high-temperature silicone rubber) to make a small pool on the top of the table. A pane of glass or Plexiglas is mounted at a slight angle above the table. As the water is heated, it forms water vapor, which condenses on the pane. Gravity pulls the condensate to the lower edge of the pane,

Students mill about the campus of the University of California, Berkeley, where the Water Pasteurization Indicator was developed.

which overhangs the pool, and drips into a trough, and then through a hose or tube into a collection jug. A still 3 feet by 6 feet large produces about 3 gallons a day in the summer, with winter production about half. The solar still is being used by the Solar Water Purification Project of the Texas State Energy Conservation Office. The El Paso Solar Energy Association (EPSEA) runs this project. EPSEA's demonstration project has installed solar stills at a colonia along the Texas-Mexico border. The colonia residents have truck-delivered water that is stored in 55-gallon drums. The solar still treats this water to provide good tasting drinking water that the children will drink. EPSEA estimates that a single still costs between $200 and $300 and requires basic tools for installation. EPSEA will provide free plans for nonprofit organizations and nongovernmental organizations (NGOs). A commercial product is available from Aqua del Sol, of Pima, Arizona. Free plans are also available from the SolarDome's School of Solar Thermal Energy web site.

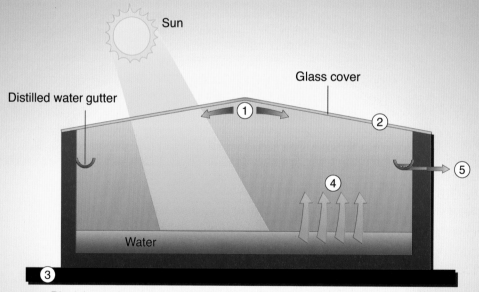

How a Solar Water Still Purifies Water

Sun

Glass cover

Distilled water gutter

Water

Black heat-absorbant surface

1. Condensed droplets flow along the inside of the glass cover and collect in the gutter.
2. A glass cover allows sunlight into the still and traps heat.
3. A black heat-absorbant surface helps to heat the water.
4. Heated by the sun, water evaporates and condenses. This process purifies the water.
5. Purified water flows to a collection jug.

Source: www.commonwealthknowledge.net

A somewhat more complex method has been developed by the PAX World Service: a flow-through unit. Using a standard solar box cooker, they added about 50 feet of black plastic tubing; a storage tank for untreated water; a prefilter (sand, gravel, and charcoal); and a thermostatic valve and container on the treated side. Since the tubing only contains about one-half gallon (1.5 liters), it is rapidly heated to the valve opening temperature of 182 [degrees] F (83.5 [degrees] C) (a mass-produced automotive radiator thermostat valve is used). As the heated water drains into the container, untreated water is drawn into the tubing. When the untreated water reaches the valve, the valve closes. This device has two main advantages over the solar box or still. Potable water is available throughout the day, depending upon the amount of solar heat. Also, the process is automatic; no

"pot-watching" is required, and there is no guessing about when the water has reached pasteurization. The device has been successfully field tested by PAX World Service and the Pakistan Council of Appropriate Technology, showing yields of 4 to 6 gallons (20 liters) a day. It costs about $50.

Although the PAX system is a distinct improvement on the solar box or still, it does not produce enough water for a village. Solar devices often use heat exchangers to increase efficiency. Heat exchangers preheat the untreated water with the heat from the treated water. As a result, output can be increased by about 400 percent, or 20 to 25 gallons (80 to 96 liters) per day. A tubular or flat metal plate can be used as the heat exchanger. Another benefit is that the outflow of treated water is much cooler than with the PAX device, so that the chance of burns is reduced. Devices that use heat exchangers are marketed by Safe Water Systems. The *Kathmandu Post* reported that the Liver Foundation Nepal is interested in working with the Friendly Appropriate Solar Technology, a California company, to manufacture these devices in Kathmandu [, Nepal]. . . .

Successful installation of any of these methods requires that the users also receive instruction on sanitary waste disposal; proper containers for water storage, transport, and dispensing; and maintenance of the system. Some past efforts at chlorine disinfection have failed because of a lack of training and the high maintenance required by those systems. Most of the developers of the systems discussed here have emphasized the need for education and are looking for NGOs and other relief organizations that can use the systems, especially where electricity and fuel are scarce and expensive. This brief overview of the various types of solar-powered water disinfection devices only touches upon the opportunities for their use in developing countries.

Facts About Solar Power

The sun is the origin of nearly every form of energy that humans use. Fossil fuels, for example, come from ancient organisms, which depended on the sun for survival. Wind energy is the result of the uneven heating of Earth's surface by the sun. Solar power technology uses sunlight to heat water or make electricity. The only major exceptions are geothermal energy, which comes from the interior heat of Earth, and tidal energy, which is mainly the result of the moon's gravitational pull on the oceans.

Solar energy can be used directly, as when solar panels convert the sun's rays into heat or electricity, or passively, as when a building is constructed so that its surfaces absorb sunlight during winter to warm the inside and reflect it during the summer. The sun's rays also can be concentrated by reflectors on a boiler to produce steam for heat or mechanical energy.

Solar generation of electricity grew more than seventyfold from 1985 to 2005. During that time installed solar cells around the world went from a capacity of 21 megawatts to 1,460 megawatts. Solar panels supplied electric power to more than 1.6 million U.S. households in 2004.

Solar Cells

Solar cells—also called photovoltaic cells—consist of layers of silicon that have different properties. When sunlight strikes a cell, it frees some electrons (see The Photovoltaic Effect). They begin to flow from the positively charged layers toward the negatively charged layers. These electrons are captured in wires running through the cell and flow out of the cell in a direct electric current.

The Photovoltaic Effect

In 1868 William Gryllis Adams and Richard Evans Day discovered that selenium produced electricity when exposed to sunlight. Today, we refer to electricity produced directly from sunlight as the photovoltaic effect. Selenium, which produces a weak electrical charge, was eventually replaced with silicon, which produces more electricity per square inch.

The Cost of Solar Generation

The cost of solar panels has steadily declined. From the mid-1970s to the mid-1990s, the average cost of an installed photovoltaic system dropped from about fifty dollars per watt to about five dollars per watt. Even so, the cost of solar-produced electricity remains four to five times higher than conventionally generated electricity.

Environmental Impacts

Solar energy is green energy, meaning that it is nonpolluting. It requires no mining or drilling, and it does not generate radioactive or other hazardous waste. However, critics point out that to provide a significant fraction of the world's electricity, solar panels would have to cover a vast area of land, which could damage the environment. Because they would require so much space, large solar facilities would have to be located in rural areas; hundreds of miles of transmission lines would then have to be run from the facilities to the cities that need power, thereby marring the landscape.

Glossary

absorber: A blackened surface on a collector that absorbs solar radiation and converts it into heat energy.

alternating current (AC): Electricity that switches direction many times each second. AC allows for transmission over long distances with comparatively little loss in power. (See also **direct current.**)

alternative energy: Energy sources different from those in widespread use at the moment. Alternative energy usually means nonpolluting forms such as solar, wind, wave, tidal, and geothermal energy. (See also **green energy** and **renewable energy.**)

collector: An insulated device, such as a rooftop panel, that collects solar radiation and converts it into heat that can warm air or liquid flowing through it.

concentrator: A lens or reflector that focuses the sun's rays on an absorbent surface to maximize the available heat in a small area.

cycles per second: In electricity, the number of times an AC circuit reverses direction.

direct current (DC): The type of electric current solar cells generate. It flows continuously in one direction, losing power as it travels over long distances. (See also **alternating current** and **inverter.**)

efficiency: The ratio of output power in electricity to the input power in sunlight, usually expressed as a percentage.

flat plate collector: A solar collector consisting of an insulated, flat, boxlike container covered with one or more layers of glass. When placed on a rooftop and exposed to the sun, its interior heats up, allowing air or a liquid circulating through it to carry the heat into the building below.

fuel cell: A technology used to generate electricity directly from gas through an electrochemical process. It can be fueled by hydrogen derived from water that is broken down by electricity generated by solar cells.

generation: The conversion of other forms of energy into electricity through the use of equipment. Generation is usually measured in kilowatt-hours.

green energy: A popular term for energy produced from renewable energy resources. (See also **renewable energy**.)

heat exchanger: A mechanism or material, such as copper tubing, that is used transfer the heat in a collector from one medium to another.

hertz: A measure of frequency in AC. (See **cycles per second**.)

inverter: A device for converting direct current, such as that generated by solar cells, into alternating current, suitable for long-distance transmission.

kilowatt: A thousand watts. (See **watt**.)

kilowatt-hour: A unit of energy equal to the work done by a kilowatt over a period of one hour. Often abbreviated as "kWh."

megawatt: A million watts. (See **watt**.)

parabolic mirror: A curved mirror shaped as a parabola to concentrate the sun's rays on a target point.

passive solar heating: The use of sunlight falling on a building's surfaces to heat the interior. Careful design and positioning of a building, along with strategic use of glass, ensures that sunlight in the winter months will warm the building but will be deflected during the summer.

photovoltaic cell: A solar generation device that makes use of thin layers of silicon to convert sunlight into electricity. The sunlight striking the cell knocks loose electrons that are induced to flow in a direct current. (See also **solar cell**.)

radiation: The flow of energy through space via electromagnetic waves, such as visible light. The sun's energy reaches Earth as radiation, which can be converted to other forms such as heat or electricity.

renewable energy: Energy derived from resources that are naturally regenerated, such as flowing water or wind.

solar cell: A silicon-based device that converts a portion of the radiant energy of sunlight into electric energy. (See also **photovoltaic cell**.)

solar energy: Energy derived from the sun, either directly as heat or indirectly as electricity. Many other forms of energy—such as coal, wind, and hydroelectric—can be traced back ultimately to the sun, but these are not generally included in the term.

solar engine: A mechanical device that operates on steam generated by heat from the sun.

solar panel: A cluster of solar cells arranged in a panel that can be oriented toward the sun.

transformer: A mechanism that transfers AC current from one circuit to another with a change of voltage in the transfer.

trough: A reflector shaped like a section of a pipe. It concentrates sunlight along a line rather than at a point.

volt: A measure of electrical potential difference. One volt is the potential difference in charge needed to make one ampere of electrons flow.

watt: An internationally recognized measure of electrical energy. A typical lightbulb requires sixty watts of electrical power.

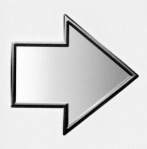

Chronology

B.C.

ca. 6000
Early magnifying glasses are used to start fires.

ca. 212
Greek mathematician Archimedes reputedly arranges hexagonal bronze reflectors to concentrate the sun's light on invading Roman ships and burns the fleet.

ca. 180
Greek scientist Diocles creates the first parabolic mirror to concentrate the sun's rays.

A.D.

20
Ancient Chinese texts record the use of mirrors to focus sunlight to ignite torches for religious purposes.

100
Roman historian Pliny the Younger takes advantage of solar heating by building a home with glass panes to keep the heat in and the cold out.

ca. 1300
Anasazi Indians in the Southwest region of North America build their homes in south-facing cliffs that take advantage of the warming power of the winter sun.

1695
Frenchman Georges Buffon uses mirrors to concentrate sunlight to a new high point; the resulting heat is capable of melting lead.

1700
French chemist Antoine Lavoisier arranges lenses to focus the sun's rays on a point that reaches more than 3,000°F, hot enough to melt platinum.

1767
Swiss scientist Horace de Saussure builds what is thought to be the world's first solar collector capable of being used to cook food.

1839
French scientist Edmond Becquerel discovers that light shining on metallic solution can induce a weak electric current that becomes known as the photovoltaic effect.

1861
French scientist Auguste Mouchout invents a solar engine that uses sunlight to generate steam for mechanical power.

1872
Swiss-born engineer John Ericsson invents a solar-powered irrigation pump for American farmers, but it fails to catch on.

1878
Mouchout displays a new and improved solar motor at the Paris Exhibition; after a three-year review, the French government declares it a technical failure.

1885
British inventor Charles Tellier creates a solar-powered pump.

1891
Baltimore inventor Clarence Kemp patents the first commercial solar water heater.

1897
Kemp's water heaters gain widespread acceptance among homeowners in sunny Pasadena, California.

1899
Inventor Aubrey Eneas, after years of work in his Boston lab, patents a solar motor.

1908
William J. Bailey of the Carnegie Steel Company invents the prototype of the modern rooftop solar collector, consisting of an insulated box with copper coils running through it.

1954
Practical solar generation is first conducted at Bell Labs when researchers Daryl Chapin, Calvin Fuller, and Gerald Pearson develop the silicon photovoltaic cell; the International Solar Energy Society (ISES) is founded.

1955

The first solar cell technologies for commercial use go on the market, but the high costs of the cells discourage most consumers.

ca. 1955

Architect Frank Bridgers designs the world's first commercially viable solar-heated office building.

1956

Plans for using solar cells to power satellites get underway at the U.S. Signal Corps Laboratories and RCA Labs.

1958

The first solar cells in space are launched aboard various U.S. and Soviet satellites.

1962

Solar cells enable *Telstar*, the first U.S. communications satellite, to begin relaying phone calls from orbit.

1963

Japan installs an array of solar cells on a lighthouse; at 242 watts, it is the world's largest photovoltaic generator to date.

1973

Skylab, an orbiting laboratory housing several astronauts, is launched, carrying with it the largest array of solar cells yet put into space; one solar panel is lost to damage during launch, but a later repair mission enables the lab to function until 1979; public interest in solar energy soars as oil shortages brought about by an international boycott cause an energy crisis; responding to the energy crisis, Sandia National Laboratories opens a solar research division.

1974

The federal government establishes the Solar Energy Research Institute; the nation's largest state solar research center is established at the University of Central Florida.

1977

President Jimmy Carter installs solar panels on the White House as an example to the nation.

1979
The second international oil embargo begins, driving oil prices up. Producers of solar technologies establish the Solar Energy Industries Association.

1980
Researchers at the University of Delaware develop the first solar cell capable of breaking the 10 percent efficiency barrier.

1991
President George H.W. Bush directs the U.S. Department of Energy to establish the National Renewable Energy Laboratory, incorporating the Solar Energy Research Institute.

1992
Researchers at the University of South Florida create a thin-film solar cell capable of generating electricity at nearly 16 percent efficiency.

1996
The U.S. Department of Energy establishes the National Center for Photovoltaics to further research into solar cells.

2002
President George W. Bush has "building-integrated photo-voltaics" installed as backup solar electric generators at the White House, replacing the solar panels Carter had installed.

2006
California undertakes a ten-year solar initiative intended to foster the installation of a million rooftop solar generators capable of producing three thousand megawatts of electricity. It is the largest solar program to date in U.S. history.

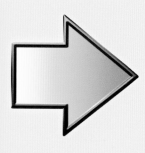

For Further Reading

Books

Daniel M. Berman, *Who Owns the Sun? People, Politics, and the Struggle for a Solar Economy*. White River Junction, VT: Chelsea Green, 1996.

G.Z. Brown, *Sun, Wind & Light: Architectural Design Strategies*. New York: J. Wiley & Sons, 2001.

Daniel D. Chiras, *The Homeowner's Guide to Renewable Energy: Archieving Energy Independence Through Solar, Wind, Biomass and Hydropower*. Gabriola, BC: New Society, 2006.

————, *The Solar House: Passive Heating and Cooling*. White River Junction, VT: Chelsea Green, 2002.

D. Yogi Goswami, *Principles of Solar Engineering*. Philadelphia: Taylor & Francis, 2000.

M.A. Green, *Third Generation Photovoltaics: Advanced Solar Energy Conversion*. New York: Springer, 2005.

International Energy Association, *Solar Energy Houses: Strategies, Technologies, Examples*. 2nd ed. London: James & James, 2003.

Thomas R. Jacobson, *Going Solar: How to Add Passive Solar Heating to Your Home*. Albert Lea, MN: Reid, 1983.

James Kachadorian, *The Passive Solar House: Using Solar Design to Heat & Cool Your Home*. White River Junction, VT: Chelsea Green, 1997.

Frank Kryza, *The Power of Light: The Epic Story of Man's Quest to Harness the Sun*. New York: McGraw-Hill, 2003.

Ralph Nansen, *Sun Power: The Global Solution for the Coming Energy Crisis*. Ocean Shores, WA: Ocean, 1995.

John Perlin, *From Space to Earth: The Story of Solar Electricity*. Ann Arbor, MI: Aatec, 1999.

Adi Pieper, *The Easy Guide to Solar Electric.* Santa Fe, NM: ADI Solar, 2001.

Dan Ramsey, *The Complete Idiot's Guide to Solar Power for Your Home.* New York: Alpha, 2002.

John Schaeffer and Sim Van der Ryn, *A Place in the Sun: The Evolution of the Real Goods Solar Living Center.* White River Junction, VT: Chelsea Green, 1997.

Madanjeet Singh, *The Timeless Energy of the Sun for Life and Peace with Nature.* San Francisco: Sierra Club, 1998.

Scott Sklar, *Consumer Guide to Solar Energy: Easy and Inexpensive Applications for Solar Energy.* Chicago: Bonus, 1995.

Solar Energy International, *Photovoltaics: Design and Installation Manual.* Gabriola, BC: New Society, 2004.

Periodicals

Martin Bond, "Solar Energy: Seeing the Light," *Geographical,* November 2000.

Duane Chapman and Jon D. Erickson, "Residential Rural Solar Electricity in Developing Countries," *Contemporary Economic Policy,* November 2, 1995.

Aimee Cunningham, "Sun and Sand: Dirty Silicon Could Supply Solar Power," *Science News Online,* September 10, 2005. www.sciencenews.org.

Belle Dumé, "A New Type of Solar Cell," *Physics Web,* November 4, 2004. http://physicsweb.org.

Robert A. Freling, "Solar Vision," *International Journal of Humanities and Peace,* November 1, 2001.

X. Gong and M. Kulkarni, "Design Optimization of a Large Scale Rooftop Photovoltaic System," *Solar Energy,* March 2005.

Glenn Hamer, "Solar Power 2002," *World and I,* June 2002.

Sharice Low, "Take Your Bedroom Off the Grid," *Home Power,* August/September 1997. www.solarenergy.org.

John S. Manuel, "Solar Flair," *Environmental Health Perspectives,* July 2003.

D. Mills, "Advances in Solar Thermal Electricity Technology," *Solar Energy*, January/March 2004.

Wahila Minshall, "Women's PV Workshop: Education That Gives & Receives," *Home Power*, December 2003/January 2004. www.solarenergy.org.

Kwabena Osei, "Solar Energy Made Simple," *New African*, December 2003.

Joshua M. Pearce, "Photovoltaics—a Path to Sustainable Futures," *Futures*, April 2002.

Joshua Radoff, "NYPV Blue: From Highrises to Brownstones, Solar Power Finds a Home in New York City," *Alternatives Journal*, Winter 2004.

Web Sites

American Society of Mechanical Engineers (www.asme.org). The American Society of Mechanical Engineers (ASME) is a 120,000-member professional organization focused on technical, educational, and research issues of the engineering and technology community. ASME conducts one of the world's largest technical publishing operations, holds numerous technical conferences worldwide, and offers hundreds of professional development courses each year. Its site includes a section on solar energy.

American Solar Energy Society (www.ases.org). The American Solar Energy Society (ASES) is the U.S. branch of the International Solar Energy Society. A nonprofit organization, ASES is dedicated to the development and adoption of renewable energy in all its forms, especially solar. Its site includes a guide to tours of solar homes and a link to its periodical *Solar Today*.

California Public Utilities Commission (www.cpuc.ca.gov). The California Public Utilities Commission is a branch of state government that regulates privately owned utilities and telecommunications. Its site includes a wealth of information about the California Solar Initiative, the nation's biggest solar project.

Database of State Incentives for Renewable Energy (www.dsire usa.org). The Database of State Incentives for Renewable Energy

(DSIRE) is a comprehensive source of information on state, local, utility, and selected federal incentives to promote renewable energy. The site has a clickable map to guide users to local incentives.

International Solar Energy Society (www.ises.org). The International Solar Energy Society (ISES) is a United Nations–accredited nongovernmental organization. It promotes the advancement of renewable energy technology, especially solar technology, in more than fifty countries around the world. Its site includes information on its activities and publications.

National Center for Photovoltaics (www.nrel.gov/ncpv). The National Center for Photovoltaics (NCPV) is a branch of the U.S. Department of Energy. Its mission is to promote development of photovoltaics in the United States by performing world-class research and development, linking partners together, and serving as a forum and information source for the photovoltaics community. The site includes extensive information about research projects.

Office of Energy Efficiency and Renewable Energy (www.eere. energy.gov). The Office of Energy Efficiency and Renewable Energy is a division of the U.S. Department of Energy. Its Web site includes considerable information about its Solar Energy Technologies program, one of eleven renewable energy programs within the office.

Solar Energy Industries Association (www.seia.org). The Solar Energy Industries Association (SEIA) is the national trade association of solar energy manufacturers, dealers, distributors, contractors, installers, architects, consultants, and marketers. Its site includes historical information on the development of solar energy and its industry, as well as information about a variety of contemporary solar technologies.

Solar Impulse (www.solar-impulse.com). The Solar Impulse project is a privately financed international effort to draw attention to the promise of solar energy by designing, building, and flying an airplane capable of taking off and flying around the world entirely under the power of its solar cells. The site includes extensive information about the project and its personnel.

Index

Adams, William, 23–25
air conditioners, solar, 86–87
alternative energy, 65
ancient world, 16–18
Andreatta, Dale, 104

Barber, Dave, 11
Barnett, Alan, 76
Barrett, Fred, 104
Basic Energy Sciences
  Advisory Committee
  (BESAC), 61
Bayon, Ricardo, 66
Becquerel, Antoine-Cesar, 18
Becquerel, Edmond, 18, 42
Berman, Elliot, 34
Borkowski, Liz, 46
Business Week (magazine), 9

Caesar, Tiberius, 18
carbon dioxide (CO_2), 46
Carey, John, 9
Carter, Jimmy, 65
central receivers (solar
  towers), 40, 42
China, 72–73
climate change, 46
  see also global warming
coal
  China's use of, 72
  costs of electricity from, 63
Coast Guard, use of solar
  power by, 34–35
Cogan, Lucy, 16

Colmey, John, 83
Crabtree, George, 60
Czochralski process, 19

Darkwa, Osei, 67, 69
Day, Richard Evans, 30
Department of Energy, U.S.
  (DOE), 60, 61
  research spending
    on hydrogen power, 13
    on solar energy, 65
  on sales of photovoltaic
    cells, 10
developing nations
  economics of, 71–72
  environmental benefits of,
    73
  power grids are insufficient
    for, 70–71
  PVC efficiency and, 50
  unsafe drinking water in,
    103
    solar solutions to, 104–109
  use of solar-generated elec-
    tricity in, 37
Done, Jonathan, 79

electricity, 63
  see also photovoltaic energy
Electronics Weekly (magazine),
  10
*Elevation of Water with the
  Solar Atmosphere* (Tellier),
  26

Elmore, Rick, 81–82
El Paso Solar Energy
  Association (EPSEA),
  107–108
Eneas, Aubrey, 28
Ericsson, John, 26–28

global warming, 8–9, 47
  as serious threat, 49
Gress, Mary, 65
Grylls, William, 30
Guzzo, Lou, 56

Hayden, Howard C., 12
heat collectors, 41–42
Hospers, John, 52
housing
  solar-hydrogen, 90–91
  solar power, 78
    barriers to mass adoption
      of, 91–92
    commercial viability, 92
    interest of homebuilders in,
      77, 79
    passive vs. active, 39
    typical customer for, 81–82
hydrogen/hydrogen power,
  12–13
  for nighttime energy needs,
    90–91

Japan, drop in cost of solar
  energy in, 49

Kass, Stephen, 18
Kathmandu Post (newspaper),
  109
Kohn, Walter, 65
Korb, Heather, 88–89

Lewis, Nate, 59, 60, 61, 65
Little, Michael, 109
Lomer, Lloyd, 34–35

Manner, David, 10
Monitor (battleship), 26
Mouchout, Auguste, 21, 29
  solar motor of, 22–23

Nansen, Ralph H., 94
Napoleon III, 23
National Aeronautics and
  Space Administration
  (NASA), 98–99
natural gas, costs of electricity
  from, 63
net metering, 79–80

offshore oil wells, 34
Ohl, Russell, 18
Oliver, Mike, 52
Osei, Kwabena, 11

parabola, 27
parabolic dishes, 40, 42
parabolic trough reflectors,
  27–28, 40, 42
Patriensa (Ghana), 66
PAX World Service, 109
Peaceful Conquest of West
  Africa (Tellier), 26
Perlin, John, 30
photovoltaic cells
  cost of, 31
    are falling, 76, 80–81
  potential of, 44
  sales of, 10
  in satellites, 20, 33

for solar power satellite, 99–100
workings of, 32, 43
photovoltaic effect, 18, 42
photovoltaic energy
  batteries for storage of, 54
  costs of
    other energy sources vs., 63
    for U.S. transition to, 55–56
  global energy grid for, 62–63
  interest of homebuilders in, 77, 79
  land and construction need for, 53, 58
  packaged systems for, 79, 82
  in rural areas, 36–37
Pink, Daniel H., 12
pollution, solar power can reduce, 69–70
power grids
  developing nations and, 70–71
  global, 62–63
Provey, Joe, 75
Public Interest Energy Research Group, 85
PV cells. See photovoltaic cells

radiation, 23
Ray, Dixie Lee, 56
Reagan, Ronald, 34–35
Rolla, Trudy C., 103

Sachs, Greg, 89
satellites, solar power, 94–95
  alignment of, 100–101
  structure of, 98–99

transmitting antenna for, 101–102
  visibility of, 95–96
  vulnerability of, 102
Schaeffer, John, 76–77
Schieren, David G., 88
selenium, 30–31
  in photovoltaic cells, 18
Service, Robert F., 59
SHINE (Solar High-Impact National Energy) plan, 49–50
Siemens, Werner von, 31
silicon, in PV cells, 43
Skylab (space station), 96–97
Smalley, Richard, 65
Smith, Charles, 21
solar boxes, for water purification, 104
solar cookers, 109
Solar Decathlon, 92
solar energy
  conversion of, 21
  distributed generation system for, 91
  growth rate of, 9
  in housing
    barriers to mass adoption of, 91–92
    commercial viability of, 92
    interest of homebuilders in, 77, 79
    passive vs. active, 39
    typical customer for, 81–82
  labor cost associated with, 55
  potential of, 48
  scientists support, 61–62
  types of, 40

U.S. energy independence
and, 47–49
uses for, 54
see also photovoltaic energy
Solar Energy Industries
Association, 49
Solar Fraud, The (Hayden),
12
*Solar Heat: A Substitute for
Fuel in Tropical Countries*
(Adams), 25
solar puddles, 106–108
solar pump, 25–26
solar stills, 106–108
solar towers (central
receivers), 40, 42
Stupp, Samuel, 61, 65
subsidies, 41–42
sun, 39, 41, 53, 62

Tellier, Charles, 25–26
Teoh Siang Teik, 83–87
thermal concentrators, 42
Thompson, Nicholas, 66
transmission loss, 48
truncated-cone reflector, 23,
29

Union of Concerned
Scientists, 38
United States
costs of solar in, 55–56
energy sources in, 57
solar power potential of,
60

Vanguard satellite, 33

Washington State
Department of Ecology, 49
water, purification of
by solar boxes, 104
by solar puddles, 106
by solar stills, 106–108
water heaters, 85–86
Water Purification Indicator
(WAPI), 104–105
Widge, Vikram, 71–72
wind power, 63
World Bank, 37, 72

Yansane, Abdoulaye M., 70
Youngquist, Walter, 55

Ziegler, Hans, 33

About the Editor

Clay Farris Naff is a journalist, author, and nonprofit executive. He served as a UPI correspondent in Tokyo and later wrote a book on contemporary social change in Japan, published in 1994 by Kodansha International. After resettling in the United States, he published widely on science and religion and edited numerous Greenhaven Press titles on science and medical topics. He serves as executive director of the Lincoln Literacy Council in Lincoln, Nebraska.